MOBY DAD I

ADVENTURES IN LIVING

By

Dan Kingsley

Moby Dad, Volume I...
Adventures in Living

By: Dan Kingsley
Foreword by Michael Kingsley

Silver Quill Publishing
Spanish Fork Utah

© 2023 by E. Daniel Kingsley
Manufactured in the United States of America

Interior design and finishing by E. Daniel Kingsley
Cover Design by Michael P. Kingsley
Editing by Drollene P. Brown

ISBN   978-1-7335223-3-5
Price:$13.99

Kingsley, E. Daniel, 1949 -
Moby Dad 1: ADVENTURES IN LIVING
by Dan Kingsley
Autobiography

Foreword

My name is Michael, sixth kid of a first son, and though I don't have the seventh son's claim to fame, I am proud to present you with the chronicles of my father's family.

The stories you are about to read are all true—each and every one of them. This you must remember, or nothing that follows will seem funny, heartfelt, insightful or ridiculous. Indeed, the phrase "you can't make this stuff up" comes to mind. I know because I was there, and you can take it from the one-eyed sixth kid: Moby Dad will remind you of the best and most embarrassing parts of your family's history.

Now, with regard to the title: this book was written by a man who was a "stallion" in his day, but he has become a happy and—if he'll excuse my French—fat grandpa of 21+ grandchildren. If you want to measure the greatness of a father, whatever his ethnicity or his career path, the rearing of the grandkids is perfect evidence. And I'll tell you, each and every grandchild, from the sport-loving redhead to the one still enthralled by his/her own feet, knows that he/she is loved by Mother and Father; and each child reciprocates.

So, when you read further, you can rest assured that what you will find are examples of truth, love, hilarity and chaos of a loving family.

I wrote only this portion, and I feel privileged to be able to do so. Thanks Dad … and you're welcome for the kick in the pants.

Michael Kingsley

Dedication

This book is dedicated to my children, my grandchildren and their descendants.

Every man wants to leave his mark, to live up to some ideal and, perhaps, feel his effort has made a difference in the lives of his family. This book, and in fact this series of books, is a poor reflection of the joy my family has given me. I trust this work may anchor each child in some small way to the family that honors God, believes in true love, believes in doing good in all things, practices an honest work ethic and understands the eternal nature of family.

Unsung in these stories is their mom. I know full well the merit of her place here, the love she gave so unselfishly and the difficulty she had in dealing with me and my military life. I was often ungrateful, and she propped me up throughout my entire career. If I have failed to honor her in these stories, I do so now and without reservation. She gave me six of the most wonderful children in history and 21 grandchildren (more or less) of equal merit (and still counting).

How lucky I am.

Dan Kingsley

TABLE OF CONTENTS

On Family Living.................................9

On Love.......................................67

Thoughts on Life in the Army.........................97

Holidays......................................135

On the Lessons of Life...............................153

Life on the Farm................................213

Noble Thoughts...............................241

VII

Chapter 1

On Family Living

Family Panic: "The Bus Is Coming!"

Our family day starts early, in two shifts. The early shift starts around 0515, and the second, around 0545. At this hour, we respond only to life's really important stuff. During the school year, of course, our entire morning rotates around one critical event: the arrival of the bus. As you will see, getting the family out of the house and down the road with breakfast, clean clothes, the essential personal hygiene and all required school books, papers and equipment by 7:00 A.M. is no easy task.

05:45 Mom arrives cheerfully and announces the time. Each kid, in his turn, bemoans the early hour and asks cosmic questions like whether Christmas will come this year and, "Is it morning already?" There is always a crisis. If not now, then sometime soon. But at least Mom gets the blood flowing.

Nancy, age seven: "I heard you. I was awake …" She props up on one elbow, eyes shut tight, hair like Phyllis Diller.

"Why is the room so dark?" Her eyes crack open, and she peeks out at her bleak world. She says she's sick, and she says she has to stay home today. She throws herself back on her pillow and covers her head with her blanket.

Do you get the picture?

Anyway, Mom hits the kitchen for lunches and checks to be sure the older kids (first shift) are already out and in pursuit of the day. She actually hums. I have heard it.

06:15 This is Mom's intermediate check. The family train picks up speed. The kids on this day are doing okay, except Nikki. She is a little late and will miss her bus if she doesn't hurry. Oh yeah, and Nancy, who is still trapped by her attack bedclothes. Mom motivates them. Nancy catapults out of bed. Nikki plods ahead.

06:45 Mom's marching orders are issued with crisp finality.

"Hustle, girls, the bus will be here any time. Mikie, brush your teeth. Nancy, what did you do to your hair? Go get a brush. Elizabeth, help Nancy find that brush, will you? Nikki! Get out! Your bus just passed the corner. You'll have to run to catch it on the other side of the circle. Let's go!"

They scatter quickly.

The house rumbles with the shuffling of feet, papers, books and other such sounds of getting ready for school. Today we are not that late, so the panic does not set in until the dreaded "B" word is issued from the kitchen.

06:55 "Bus!"

Mom is standing kitchen sentry duty, at the ready and braced for the onslaught. She has heard the bus and is ready to solve each new crisis as it arises.

You can hear the house fall suddenly silent as each kid stops all movement to strain for the familiar sounds of that old bus chugging up our street. It can't be here already. Surely, Mom is wrong.

Beth: "Bus?"

Nancy: "The bus?"

Mikie: "The bus!"

The stunning realization strikes all of them at once, as though it is a complete surprise. The stampede begins. In unison, they yell:

"The Bus!"

With one mind, every kid makes a last grab for his papers, slings the book bag onto his back, grabs a jacket and makes for the kitchen.

Today is still a good day. So far, no critical problems have arisen. In the kitchen Mom, prepared for any action, is involved in trying to pass the right lunch or money or some combination of the two to each kid.

Nancy has left her lunch pail at school, so her sandwiches are hastily jammed into a bag on top of the chips. Mom mourns at the lost cause that is Nancy's hair. It bears a strange resemblance to the hair on someone who has kissed a light socket. Mom gives Nancy a hug and sends her off.

Mikie runs out with his backpack on, but with his jacket on one arm because he can't get it over his pack. He streaks through the kitchen and grabs his lunch pail off the counter. It flies open, spilling all contents. He stops and looks toward the door, then at his lunch, then the door. He seems paralyzed by indecision. Mom leaps to gather all the lunch within reach. Throwing it into the pail, she shuts it on Mikie's little finger. He wails. Mom consoles, then gives it a quick kiss, and he is off.

Elizabeth now calmly reminds Mom that she needs a permission slip signed before she can be allowed to go on her school outing today.

Mama keeps her cool.

"Where is it?"

"You must have it, Mom, 'cause I gave it to you." Bethy smiles.

Mom mumbles something about murder as she frantically searches for the missing document.

The bus now has stopped out front. The panic has been replaced with a frenzied family determination to get everybody on board before it leaves. One kid limps out just in time, so the bus actually stops. One kid then stumbles out the door, just in time to delay the bus a little while longer, but slowly enough to let Mom make up another permission slip. At last, Elizabeth is out the door and makes it to the bus. And Mom is left standing alone among the debris. She is tired. Very tired.

If you recite this little story at double-time in concert with the William Tell Overture, you may get a better feel for the event.

Things of the Moment

It is a grave paradox that the nature of man requires him to work so hard to accomplish things of the moment, without giving thought to things of eternal merit.

How often I look at my independent young son and wish I might share those first few years with him again.

Show and Tell

One day after I returned from work Michael, my youngest, came creeping up to me bashfully. He asked me if I were going to be busy Friday. I thought about it a moment.

I take every other Friday off (twice a month) to do work on my weekly newspaper column, but I felt I could handle anything a five-year-old could dig up. I told him I was doing something, but asked what was on his mind.

"Well, Daddy … you know Andy?"

Who doesn't? Andy is our three-legged dog, something of a celebrity since I began writing my column regularly.

"Is Andy okay?" I asked.

"Oh. Yeah. He's great. Listen, Dad. I told my teacher … well … that you could bring Andy. To school. Friday."

"Oh." I frowned appropriately. He winced.

"For Show and Tell, Dad. Can you bring him, huh Daddy?"

His little face barely held back the tears. I knew it would be tough to squeeze in time to go to the school, but not as tough as saying no.

"And just who told you I could do that, anyway? Was it your mamma again?" I winked. He burst into a grin.

"But I can't make it this Friday. Next Friday. Okay?"

Well, he nearly started doing back flips across the room. One week later, as I feared, Mike was up early and had a leash on Andy before I could get out of bed to tell him this was the wrong Friday.

Then on Monday, Andy got sick. He is allergic to fleas, you see, and he gets sores now and then that need treatment. We worried about him all week, but the vet fixed him up, good as new. We even gave him a bath, for all the good it did. But he smelled swell, for a change. Or at least he smelled somewhat better than usual.

Then Friday rolled around. Mikie danced around as though it were Christmas! He hugged me when he got up. He hugged me at breakfast. He hugged me five times before getting on his bus, reminding me every time he did that I had to be there at

9:30 A.M. sharp. He asked me over and over if I knew where his school was, and I assured him I did.

Well, 8:45 A.M. arrived and Andy seemed happy to get in the car. I had no trouble with him at all. But I got lost. It's a good thing I had started early. I made it on time, in spite of my mix-up.

With about a minute to spare, I jumped out of the car and let the dog out. I leashed him, and we hobbled into the building. I was met by a teacher who was obviously concerned about an old guy in bib overalls trying to walk into the school with an ugly dog—a three-legged dog, to boot.

The teacher dutifully tried to steer me away by asking my business, but when I said I was there for Show and Tell, she shrugged helplessly and pointed me to the office.

The principal was there looking through window, probably to judge the success of her lieutenant in getting rid of me. The horror of the principal was obvious when I walked up to the office with my dog in tow. I could almost see the words I imagined were stuck in her throat, showing on her face. Probably something like: "… dirty, homely, flea-bitten, three-legged dog and farmer … in my school …"

And I suspected her thoughts: "… disease … dog bite … dog hair …" and other yucky, litigation-worthy stuff.

For all that, she turned out to be sweet and very gracious. She eyed the dog carefully but pointed down the hall, and I wandered away.

I got lost again, if you can believe it, and went down the wrong hall. But I finally arrived at the open classroom door only two minutes late.

The teacher must have been a Marine Drill Instructor in a former life, because she had them "dress-right-dress" on the floor when I came up to the open door. Michael nearly burst out of his place, and I could see that he was about to run over to me in the doorway. The teacher had just seen me when Mike jumped up, but she was still startled to see him move so quickly.

"Mikie!" I exclaimed, "Ask your teacher!"

He looked back at his teacher sheepishly, and she nodded with a smile. He seemed awfully glad to see us. He had on the biggest grin in the world as he took my hand and led me over to a chair in the middle of the front of the classroom. I sat down, and Mike immediately put his arms around Andy. The boy really loved that old dog.

Mike was allowed to stand beside me and answer questions. All the hands went up, and Mike got really nervous. He sighed deeply several times, as though picking a classmate was a really tough chore, but he finally got into the swing of it. One at a time, he carefully answered all the questions.

How heavy is the dog?

This turned out to be the toughest question of the day. Mike seemed baffled and looked at me. I looked at him. He looked at me again, anxiously. Attempting to put the words into his mouth, I whispered, "As heavy as me."

Whereupon he announced to the bewildered class, "… as heavy as my Dad!"

"No, goofy, as heavy as you!" I spouted. They all burst into laughter, and after that, it was fun.

Q: Did he have a girlfriend?

A: No. We keep him in the yard.

Q: How do you care for him?

A: I feed him and give him clean water. He sleeps on a blanket in the room where our washing machine is.

Q: What do you feed him?

A: Dogfood.

Q: Is there something special about Andy?

A: No, he's just kind of a stinky old dog.

Q: Where does he sleep?

A: In our back room. He's an outside dog. Other than that, he is normal.

Q: Do you play with him?

A: Yeah. A lot! Well, we run around the back yard sometimes.

About this time, all the questions were done, and the teacher asked me if they could pet him. I told her he might be stinky, but that they could pet him. I said they might want to wash their hands afterward. She nodded knowingly, and had already planned for this. She lined them up to see the dog. Then she sent them to a sink in the back of the classroom where they washed their hands.

Suddenly, as a little girl was petting him, she caught her breath and exclaimed, "Why, he's missing a leg!"

That got a whole lot of attention. All the kids gathered around again.

Q: How did it happen?

A: Well, he ran away one day, and came back without it.

Q: Where? Weren't you watching him? Did it hurt?

Anyway, Andy was treated like a wounded war hero for the next ten minutes. Then it was finally over.

The teacher thanked me and reviewed the three things a dog needs besides love: food, water and exercise. The lesson was complete.

Mike, realizing I was leaving, ran over again and hugged me. As I kissed him and turned to go, I suddenly realized everyone in the room was enjoying our affection.

At that moment, I understood that the love of a wonderful son is a priceless gift, one that is the envy of all who see it.

The teacher said Mikie could show me out, so he took my hand and led me down the hall. As I stepped out the door, he yelled after me:

"Now remember, Dad, give him some fresh water when you get home."

Okay, kid. Just for you.

Fairy Tale Winker

Once upon a time, Elizabeth Jean (B.J. we call her, our #4 kid) developed a very irritating habit. She could talk forever without a breath, and she had such a cheery smile that you just hated to tell her to dry up. So one day, in a bit of jest, I began to let my right eye wink during one of her long … er … discussions.

I started with a bit of a twitch, and ended up with a mind-boggling spasm. It was sort of comical, and she finally yelled at me.

"Dad! What are you doing?"

I answered that she was obviously telling a story, because my Fairy Tale Winker was going off.

She was caught somewhere between embarrassment and anger, sputtering that I was not nice, and that surely my eye shouldn't wink over that!

But from that time forward, each time she would carry on and on, I would let a twitch escape my face, and she would giggle and quiet down.

Well Nancy (kid #5), age three, developed the same habit of talking incessantly. But with her habit came a resolute determination not to be dissuaded from her gabbing.

I remembered this old trick and began to try it on her. By the time she was four, her response was to pick out a phrase of ten or so words, in gibberish, and repeat them over and over to see if she could really get the old "winker" going.

If she were deeply involved in some major discourse, I could catch her completely off guard. A smile of embarrassment would flash across her face for a moment as she realized I had gotten her again. Then she would try like the dickens to get the old "winker" going in any way she could, usually by repeating some little meaningless phrase.

One day when Nancy was rambling on and on about something I didn't care about, I first paid no heed. Suddenly, I started the old "winker" going feverishly, clutched my eye and yelled.

"Stop! Stop it Nancy! I can't take any more!" I fell to the ground and rolled around for effect, still clinging to my beleaguered eyeball.

She was stunned. The mind of my four-year-old was instantly spun into overload, and she looked at me, first in wonder, then in aggravation.

"Dad!" she hollered. "Daddy! Stop that!" She paused a moment, initially confused. First she saw no response to her plea. But I peeked in a moment of weakness due to my curiosity to discover her mood, and she became angry.

Caught in my lie, I continued to clutch at my "stricken" eyeball, determined to get all the mileage there was left in it.

"That's no winker! Dad, I am telling you! No winker! Stop it, Daddy!"

She was out of humor this time. When she began to cry, I knew it was enough. I stood and picked her up. I told her how much I loved her but added she had to cut me some slack and ease up on her constant talking.

"After all, how much do you think ol' Dad's eye can take?"

She settled down, hugged me, and ran back to see B.J.

I didn't realize how peeved she was this time until several minutes later. She had gone into B.J.'s room and explained how she had talked me into spasms of distress. B.J. had tried to convince her that it was only play, but Nancy continued to insist that she could disable me with her magic words.

Sure enough, Nancy would not rest until she proved her point. She took B.J. in tow and dragged her into the dining room, where I had overheard the course of the whole discussion. She made B.J. stand beside my chair while she stood back a few feet and squared off, looking me directly in the eye. Then she started.

It was pure blather. No sense at all. But I stared coldly at her a full minute before allowing the first twitch out.

The first twitch encouraged her. She got louder. She looked at B.J. for approval, and she droned on. Another twitch drove her to new efforts. She talked still faster. And louder. And faster, still, she talked. Another twitch. More spasms. She talked faster. She spoke louder.

Finally, she had me in a full twitching frenzy. Surely, she would stop, I thought. But she went on and on. I seized my poor eyeball and fell to the floor again, moaning for mercy. Elizabeth was in stitches, and it made poor Nancy even more determined. She re-doubled her efforts. B.J. howled. Nancy got madder. Finally, even more tired than I, she stopped.

She threw her head back and dusted off her shirt. She looked with scorn at her poor dad on the floor, clutching his eyeball. She stared coldly at B.J. and walked proudly out of the room.

"Humph! Told ya."

Your Choice: A Hug or a Squash

I can't always give the kids the time they deserve. So when I am with a kid, I love him or her "most of all." I have explained the rules of this arrangement to the satisfaction of all parties, and it works well.

With six kids, sometimes you have to break the routine to get through, but each kid has to get his dose of love, or there are problems. At least, that's the way it is at my house.

Each morning, Mom goes through pretty much the same routine. She wakes the kids, gets them ready for school and sends them on their way. Most of the time, however, I have to wake Nancy, our little Grumpy Bear. She needs some special attention to get started that early. But on this particular day, Mom had to do it. Nancy was dug in, and when I arrived home that morning, Nancy was in rare form. She was really surly.

She just couldn't get up. Even with repeated encouragement and lecture, she could not be budged. Finally, in fear of assault by her irate mother, she had actually sat up and had become real ugly. She was rude to all visitors. She frowned. Her eyes were dark; her hair was untamed.

Please note here, I am talking "freight train, dirt road" ugly. I went into her room, and she gave me a stare that could have caused me injury. If her face had frozen in that cramp, it would have been awful.

Anyway, I sat down carefully beside her. She sat stiffly while I tried to talk to her gently. Nothing happened.

Then I reached out, got a firm hold and hugged her. I hugged and hugged. I told her I loved her; that she was special to me, and that I couldn't bear to go through the day thinking Nancy was mad at her daddy.

I had surprised her. She was not sure she was happy about this attack on her very personal space, and she decided to be mad. Real mad. Stiff as a board.

I hugged some more. She squirmed, but I held on. I told her how tough it was to show her how much I loved her because there were five other kids who needed love too, but that I had so much love to give, I hardly had time to share it. And if I didn't share it with her now, I would bust!

She stayed stiff.

I hung on. I told her I dearly loved her mama, and Nancy stiffened afresh.

"Why?" she snarled.

"Because she let me have you. She let me have all you kids. Actually, she wanted all of you, and I just helped a little."

"Really?"

"Yeah." Nancy was still stiff, but she laid her head on my shoulder now. She wiggled again, looking for an easy escape. But I held on. Time for more hugs.

I told her how much Mama loved her. I mentioned how proud we were of her reading and how foolish she had been to stay awake so late last night.

"Yeah," she said. I kissed her gently, and she put her arms around me. I hugged her again, but I knew her starving spirit was only about a quarter full now.

That would be only enough love to get her through to lunch. More hugs.

I told her how long ago before we were married, her mama and I had gone to a zoo in the early part of one winter. Mama had gone up to the camel pen and asked me if I could give a camel-call. I had laughed at her. She could, Mom had insisted.

And I told Nancy how I fell in love with her mama when she stood back and yelled, "Here, camel! Here, camel, camel!"

And four of those camels came running out of their little camel barn, in defiance of the cold weather. Four of them.

And that is when Nancy laughed.

When she did, I saw my chance. I started tickling her. I rolled over and squashed her until she was breathless. When I let her up, she was again the warm, loving little girl I knew so well.

And I told her that if she ever thought she could let me go the whole day without my Nancy-hug, she was wrong.

"A hug or a squash. That's it. You give me a hug, or I give you a squash!"

Now, Mikie, my youngest, bought into that business too. A hug or a squash. No negotiating. And it has been that way ever since.

Try it. I have found that the younger they are, the more effective is the delivery. It seems to make the heart more tender.

It certainly makes a more peaceful home.

Special Kids Are Happy Kids

In our church, we have a special section of Sunday school class called "Primary." It is for children under twelve years of age. Each Sunday a child is singled out by the primary president to be honored for his or her special qualities.

This is accomplished by a guarded process that displays these qualities in a wonderful light. First, in the black of night, the child's teacher places a secret call to the parent. A written paragraph is requested concerning the selected child. In addition, special questions are asked, such as what are his favorite colors and foods, what are the names of his animals or brothers and sisters.

On Sunday morning the teacher will play a brief game to let the children guess who is being honored by giving clues. When the child figures out who he or she is, the teacher reads the paragraph by Mom and Dad, and the child is honored by all in that solemn forum.

Well, my youngest son, Mikie, has a wonderful teacher. She really loves him. And when she called me, I wrote a nice paragraph.

I delivered the paragraph and forgot all about it. He went off to his Sunday School class, and I went off to mine. When he returned to attend our sacrament meeting later, something seemed amiss.

He still had his tie on, his shirt tucked in, and all his other "stuff" was still on (such as shoes and socks).

I was a little surprised.

"But hey, he is five, after all," I reasoned. "And he is bound to keep his tie on once in a while, isn't he?"

Anyway, he strolled up to my pew with a big smile, climbed into my lap and leaned back with a big sigh. He said nothing, just smiled that big smile. After a brief moment he turned around and hugged me. Then he sat down again, still saying nothing.

"I love you, Mike," I whispered. "You're getting almost too big to sit in my lap now, you know?"

"I know," he sighed again, contentedly.

I was baffled now, since by this time he was usually running his little talker faster than an old '33 record on a '45 speed. But as he sat quietly, he reached into his pocket and handed me a piece of paper. It had my paragraph on it, and he didn't even look to see if I would take it.

"Read this," he said quietly.

"Mike, I wrote that. I know what it says. I love you."

"It's okay, Dad, I don't mind. Read it anyway."

So I read it aloud quietly:

"Our youngest son Michael is very special to us.

He is a sweet spirit who openly shows his love for his mommy and daddy. He is eager to obey all things that are good. He sings wonderful bedtime songs to his daddy and helps Mama in the house and in the garden. He rubs Dad's back and feet, and always gives a "Mikie hug" to help his dad and mom's day go better.

He helps make peace when his brothers and sisters are not getting along. Mikie is a good and faithful friend who shares his things happily and who always tells the truth. He loves school and takes good care of our wonderful old dog.

We love Mikie very much!"

I was moved by the way Mike listened to this. He sort of leaned this way and that, as though his little soul needed to bask in the light of these things to warm up. But he said nothing.

"How did I do, Mike?"

"Good, Dad. You did real good. Read it again."

"Son, why don't you just listen to the speaker? I'll have time later."

Then with wisdom he does not comprehend, he said quietly, "You have time now, Daddy. Later I'll be too big."

I read it again.

Kids are only as special as they feel. We must remember to let them know it.

This Stuff Changes the World

The advice given on the average problem is free and probably worth a little less than the asking price. Men are labeled brilliant not because they sell their counsel, but because they can convince the payee that it is a bargain.

The stuff that changes the world, however, receives precious little attention and no money, and it is given without thought:

"Dad … can you tell me what you think about this?"

Kids Don't Need Expensive Toys

For Christmas one year I got a chair that was contained in a wonderful box. My daughter became obsessed with that box. Nancy, age 5, nagged at me, saying she needed it and wanted it, and it would make her very happy to be in possession of such a fine, sturdy box. She crooned and whined over it until I could hardly put up with her.

I didn't want her to have it because it was just more trash laying around the house. I was certain I would have to deal with it later. I would have to persuade the garbage man to take it after the Christmas grace period, and it would be cluttering up our busy home while it was being used, if ever it was used at all. I said no! And I meant it. Sort of. In a grumpy sort of way. But I never got around to throwing it out.

One day I came home and Nancy came to greet me at the door. She hugged and kissed me as though I had just returned from an overseas tour, and she thanked me for her new playhouse. Then she took my hand carefully and led me to the room where the "box" had become her dream house.

She beamed as she showed me every deluxe feature on her new little house. She had been very inventive, and her older brothers had helped. Even Mama had gotten into the act. There were roof shingles drawn on the top of it, and if she wanted more light, she just opened the little windows she had cut in the roof. It had a door with windows and handles drawn on it, and it was just big enough for a kid to get into it without any trouble. She and Mikie, her baby brother, had played all day in that box. They used it for two months before it fell apart. Then they mourned over the loss.

That reminded me of another time--another world, it seemed. About thirteen years earlier, we had another big heavy box that had become a part of the family. I don't recall how we got it, but we were broke right down to our milk money. I had been playing with our four-year-old son in our sparsely furnished living room when it occurred to me that he might enjoy playing in it.

I started making a house out of it, but I was struck with a different idea. I drew tracks on the side, made a turret out of a smaller but heavy-duty box, put a "gun" in it (made from a 2" x 24" wrapping paper cardboard tube), and presented it to Jeff as his very own tank.

Holy Cow! The kids from all over the neighborhood came to play in the thing. It was used so much for six months that it was a good thing we had very little furniture. He got a lot of wear out of it and was really mad when we wouldn't let the packers ship it to Washington.

As I think of it, most of the toys I remember as a kid were economy models. For Christmas one year, Dad rebuilt a bicycle that must have had ten coats of paint on it. It had one speed, giant tires, and brakes that worked. The only new thing on it was a thumb-operated bell. The bike was way too big, and I ran full tilt into a big cement wall and nearly killed myself on it. I had it for five years.

I belonged to the Cub Scouts when I was a kid. They sponsored a boat building contest once, and Dad was too busy to help me do much. But in a free moment, he took some steel fabric and shaped a sort of boat out of it (about as big as a bushel basket!). He covered it with duct tape, stuck a pencil in the bow and put a little flag on it. It didn't win for beauty or speed (two of the categories), but it won the cargo carrying contest. It carried everything else there. First, they put in all the marbles that were supposed to be used to load the boats. Then they put in the can that carried them. Then, one at a time, they stacked up all the other little Cub Scout boats. I was the king of boat builders!

I don't think kids need fancy toys. If they are free to use their imaginations, they will learn to wring the joy out of life naturally. Try it sometime.

Next time you are watching a bunch of kids, turn off the TV. After an hour's TV withdrawal, if they are like my kids, they will be playing together. Quietly. Happily. And when you turn that TV back on, unless they are especially bored, they will usually all go to another room to play … with a cheap toy.

On Little Boy Legends

"Don't you remember that, Dad? You know, when you jumped up on the wild cow and rode it to the store with Grandpa? Huh? Don't ya, Dad, huh?"

"Oh, that time. Sure I do. Really! Honest. Well, sort of. That was Grandpa's story. I only remember part of it. You know, son, Grandpa was always kind of silly."

Well, it is sort of funny, but kid memories are often skewed into strange proportions. They are great! But you can never go back. Reality just never seems as good as the memory.

MOBY DAD I: ADVENTURES IN LIVING

I remember my Grandma Kingsley had a small patch of really soft grass in her lawn, on a little slope, in the shade. And I would run out there and sit in it every time I went to her house.

My Grandpa Marsh had a little stream in his back yard, which Grandma kept manicured and decorated with pretty rocks and little statues. The stream ran from a spring uphill from his back yard, down under his house and out into his front yard. It flowed into two little rock-lined pools. Goldfish, huge ones, lived in those little pools. And they weren't all gold either. Some of them were spotted with gold, or patchy colored with blue and brown, sort of like a tiny pinto pony with fins. And these pools were so cold that if you dipped a toe in, it would come out pale blue.

You know, when I was a little kid, I loved those pools but was afraid to get in. My little boys ran out there one day, stripped off their pants and, to my great horror, waded in. The only bad thing that happened was their little legs were really cold.

Grandpa also had a big campfire circle out back where folks could meet and have the biggest weenie roasts. The circle was surrounded by sort of continuous stone steps, made from the stones some mason had put together. One Christmas, when my brother and I were visiting from Arizona, we sneaked out there, made our initials out of more rocks and left them there as a surprise for Grandpa and Grandma. They loved it.

Grandpa was really a cheery sort of man. He always carried two types of candy in his pockets. Cinnamon, which could burn the tongue out of a stone lion, and white (and sometimes pink) mint candies. Man, I loved those mints! I still buy those things from time to time, and Grandma still sends me a bag now and again.

Today the mints aren't nearly as good as they used to be, but they are still pretty good. I lost some of my love of them when my dad pointed at the white cakes in a urinal once and said with a laugh, "And Danny, don't eat those mints!"

Grandpa Marsh was an antique collector, and he inspired me to become interested in antiques. He once gave me an old iron with the date stamped right on the handle. You know, one of those things women in the old days used by putting it on a glowing hot stove, letting it get real hot, and then ironing sheets dampened with sprinkled water. Last time I saw it, Mom used it to prop the bathroom door open in our old house. There is no telling how many bruises that thing delivered to our tender little toes.

Grandpa had a wooden leg, and he creaked when he walked. He drank a medicinal powder called Bromo Seltzer by the gallon, I suppose because his stump hurt him so. It was a sort of Alka Seltzer in the old days, a pain killer made of powder that you put in a glass. You were supposed to put one teaspoon of powder in one glass of water, let it fizz a bit, and then you'd drink it down. Grandpa did things his way. He put about three times the powder in one third the water and downed it, and he did it often. The stuff was really sodium bromide. It was removed from the market when it was discovered to be poisonous. He died around the age of 62, if my calculations are correct. He had a cerebral hemorrhage. I am certain that either the stress of that injury or the poison of that medicine killed him.

Anyway, he had an image that a little kid really appreciated. Grandpa always smelled good, he was soft all over, and he would laugh at the drop of a pin. He had the highest tenor belly-laugh, and it made me think of Santa Claus every time he did it. (My Santa Claus always sounded like a real high tenor, you see).

He also had the neatest floppy old hat you ever saw, which I wore often.

And he had a refrigerator in the back room slam full of tiny bottles of pop. My favorite was Birch Beer, a sort of a spicy root beer. And the floor of that room was covered with bottle caps. Thousands of them! I couldn't imagine the gallons of delicious pop that had to be drunk to put them all there.

I had an Uncle Ernie (Grandpa's brother) who lived in Pennsylvania. He had a sugarbush, that is, an area of maple trees from which he collected sap and made maple syrup. In the winter, it was a dreamland of white snow and heavenly smells. He collected his sap in buckets over a huge stand of maple trees (at least, to a five-year-old, it was huge!), and he would drive the wagon around to collect it. Then he brought the sap back to the shed for boiling. It smelled so sweet, and it was warm as toast in there. It was all magic to a little kid. If you have never tried maple syrup right out of the vat, you don't know what you are missing.

At the end of the day, Ernie would collect a bit of boiling syrup which was nearly ready for bottling and pour it in the cold snow, in little strips. You could pick it right up and eat it. Wow! What I would give for some of that stuff right this minute!

Then there was my Great Grandma Myers. She was only about as tall as I, and at age five, I wasn't very tall. She had a magic potion, which I dearly loved, and she served it when I was just a wee critter. It was red and sweet and just cool enough to drink without ice. It was wonderful! She served it in a huge dining room where the whole family could eat gobs of delicious food and rich pies. Nothing has ever tasted as sweet and cool and good as that drink.

Great Grandma Myers died when she was 86, as I recall. When I was grown and in the Marine Corps overseas, I wrote my grandmother, her daughter, to get me the recipe for that drink. I had no clue how hard it would be to make or prepare, but I was ready for a bit of home and willing to do what had to be done. She immediately responded with an envelope, but I was in the field and could not get to it for a couple days. So when I got to the mailroom, I was really excited.

I got it and ran away to open my prize, this recipe from home, a part of my past. It was a thick envelope, and I expected a glorious taste of home in that wonderful letter. I opened it up to discover that magic must be included in all the best things to make them really good.

It was a nickel packet of cherry Kool Aid.

Wanted: Ten Eagles

For the third year in a row, I have been … well … I have been offered the opportunity to work for the local Boy Scouts in their annual money-making event.

I have two Boy Scouts who became Eagle Scouts in Troop 23, Ozark, Alabama. Now I have another young man who is impatiently tramping down that path to jump into the fray right behind them. So, not only do I want to, but I feel I owe it to the Troop as a sort of debt of honor.

Now, this is no ordinary Boy Scout event. Well, is there ever any ordinary Boy Scout event? Anyway, our project is known all over the Tri-States (Alabama, Florida, Georgia). In fact, you may have stood in line outside our booth at the National Peanut Festival, in Dothan, Alabama, as many others have done, in rain, freezing cold, wilting heat and gladly waited your turn to dive into a big, fat, cinnamon dipped, sodium-, saturated fat- and cholesterol-laden, sugar-coated elephant ear.

What? You have never heard of an elephant ear? Really? What a shame. Such a treat is nearly unknown up north. Or out west.

Well, you needn't conjure up a vision of earless elephants. This delicious treat is a large, floppy, doughnut-like concoction that has held the Wiregrass spellbound for years. It looks like an elephant ear, but it tastes like manna from Heaven.

The story is an old one, and as near as I can piece it together, here goes. Years ago, the local Boy Scouts for a Church of Jesus Christ of Latter-Day Saints (LDS) organization in Dothan developed a money-making project by selling the forerunner of the current elephant ear. They bought a cheap trailer from which to sell it, put in some deep fat fryers, laid in a huge stock of sugar and started. They had some mediocre success with it each year for a while, but nothing to brag about.

Basically, the elephant ear was made like this: You took a huge, thin, flap-jack-like piece of dough, slung it into some boiling grease, dipped the thing in sugar, and there you had it—a sweet bread with no redeemable nutritional or social value whatsoever.

One day a furener (nope, not a foreigner; he was a furener, that is, a Yankee from a strange place a bit further north than Montgomery, like New York City) stopped in and started talking to a Scouter in the booth. It turned out he was some know-it-all chef from a fancy restaurant. He had in his hands a stale elephant ear from the night before. As he talked, he would taste it and make comments. He correctly estimated the elements and the proportions of the recipe, to the astonishment of the guy in charge of the booth. The chef then pronounced it delinquent in this ingredient and that ingredient in certain proportions until he had re-invented the elephant ear recipe. The Scouter took faithful notes and prepared to consider them when the chef recommended they add cinnamon to the sugar. The Scouter was immediately impressed that this just might be worth a try.

Well, the organization has changed a lot from then until now, and today there are between nine and 13 Scout Troops involved each year in manning this booth. Ten people (usually parents, and this is the minimum crew) run the booth, and when the crowds gather, the frenzy in the booth is "Katy bar the door" until the festival closes each night.

This secret concoction has become the rage of the festival. And it is successful beyond any normal expectations. Each night and during the day shifts, it requires six hours of hard volunteer work. Usually each parent works at least two nights during the festival. And that does not count the clean-up shift, which is the least fun and most challenging.

Each work shift starts out happily. All the volunteers greet and move to their assigned crew. There is the mixing crew, which makes up the dough, cuts it into portions, mashes it into patties, and passes it to all the cooking crews. The cooking crews assigned to each vat carefully place the dough in the grease; when the fried dough is removed, it is then covered it with sugar and cinnamon. Then there are the hawkers. Yes, that is what they are called … two inside to hand them out, and at least two outside to sell them. Mix all this up, get about 30 folks in line, get the mixing crew a little behind, and you have well organized, panicked chaos, just as with any other Boy Scout project.

You should see the clean-up shift. Sugar, grease and gooey flour cover the counters, the equipment and the floor, every square inch of it. The floor is so slick from grainy sugar that you have to take care not to fall in it. Once the crew starts sweeping up, great clouds of flour and sugar fill the air, all the windows have to be open and the place vented. The grease, which covers everything, is washed off with hot water and soap, creating still more slop until it is mopped and cleaned up.

So, this begs the question. Why do they do this? The money, every cent, goes to someone else. They socialize, it is true. And they enjoy the work, it is also true. And they get a free elephant ear from time to time. But why bother?

Believe me, I know why.

Any parent would give their fortune for the well-being of their children. And I know what the Boy Scouts means to my family. Scouts make good citizens, good husbands and fathers, good leaders, good men. Society needs them. But I know how easy it is to distract a boy into the wrong things, and how important it is that I participate in his progress.

And I suppose it would be just too bold to hang out this sign:

"Wanted: 10 Eagle Scouts. Throw money."

Fur

My wife and I had wanted a little piece of farmland for years. I ended up buying a 14-acre place that was crowned with the biggest mistake of our marriage: a small, used, doublewide mobile home.

Now don't take offense, ye salespersons of "manufactured homes," but the mean wife, six kids and the three-legged dog launched a frontal assault on that place that could have taken

Europe in a month. I admit the contest was unfair, but that old trailer allowed us to have a wonderful place in the country. Anyway, that's another story.

One of the many things I loved about this trailer was the absolute absence of privacy. I mean, you could take two steps at one end of the trailer and someone would feel both steps at the other end. And the living room was so small that if anything was left on the floor there, it would be stepped on in the night.

So on this particular night my deep sleep was interrupted by something I thought was a restless kid. If you're a mom or dad, you can recognize that little whine before the shriek when your kid is trying to wake up. I heard something, and about the time I knew I was awake … thump!

I recognized the sound immediately. My youngest daughter, age three, had jumped out of bed and would be coming.

I dozed for a moment, then I woke again. Thump … plop … plop … plop …She was making her way through the trailer to our room. Our bathroom light was on, so she could find our room easily. No need to get up… and I was gone … zzzzzzzz.

Splash! The familiar rolling of the waves in our cheap, giant, economy size waterbed roused me again for a brief moment as Nancy dived in. She snuggled against my back as she does when she's either cold or scared. She's a little restless tonight, I remember thinking … zzzzzzzz.

ON FAMILY LIVING

A tiny arm reached up and over my chest, tickling me. I squeezed her hand, thinking she just needed a little reassurance … zzzzzzzz.

Now little fingers began playing with my pajama top. Little searching fingers, wandering around my neck, playing with my chest hairs. I cleared my throat, aggravated by the interruption, prepared to fix the problem … then the little fingers patted me. Okay, they seemed to say, it's okay. Time to sleep … zzzzzzzz

Pain! A sharp pain jolted me awake. Agony! Oh, how it hurt! My upper torso seemed to be on fire! I clutched my chest and rolled into a little ball, yelling as loudly as I possibly could, trying to muster all the assets I could bring to bear on this pain!

I sat up in a daze, trying to figure out how bad it was. It was 2 A.M. It didn't seem to hurt so much now. In fact, rubbing it seemed to help. As a matter of fact, it seemed to hurt right there.

I looked around me to find Nancy sitting up in bed next to me, wide-eyed terror on her face.

"Mama! Mama!" she cried.

I reached to comfort her, thinking I had scared her, and she drew away. I leaned farther to reach her and ease her fear. There, in the glow of the bathroom light, I saw the answer—a dozen curly chest hairs clutched in her tiny fist.

She had settled down by now. I mean, the beast had stopped roaring, and she had no reason to fear for her life. Mom had raised herself to one elbow by now and was wondering what was going on. Nancy looked at me, then at the treasured possessions she held tightly in her fist, then at Mom, and whispered in awe…

"Mama! Daddy has … fur!"

Things of Eternal Merit

What is truly significant in the current moment? Look back to the years and just try to remember what was so important at that time. Boss? Associates? How about friends, reports, career development? How much of what you do is really what you will always consider important?

Ask your sons or daughters. Somehow the mind of a child can pick out the long-term value of each moment.

"Dad, remember when we …?"

For a Moment of Privacy

In a house with six kids (or more), privacy has a special place, and that place is hard to find at times.

For example, my oldest daughter turned twelve, and my sweet wife dutifully brought home something we graciously call a "trainer bra." For any of you unequipped with the software required for this item of apparel, or for anyone who simply has no idea what it is, it resembles two eye-patches sewn onto a cloth harness. It has two purposes:

1. It announces the advent of blossoming womanhood, and

2. It prepares the wearer for its appropriate use.

The arrival of this equipment was, overnight, a landmark experience for my three girls, ages 12, nine and seven. Within days of its arrival, my seven-year-old stood in her bedroom, defiant, arms crossed, and told Dad to leave, or "… you'll see my bosoms!"

Mikie, my four-year-old, wandered innocently into their bedroom one day and was greeted by the shrieks of anger and dismay. He stood there confused by the change from (literally) yesterday, when no one cared, and he started yelling. I ran in to see what was wrong, just as he turned to leave. He looked at me, disgusted, and said, "C'mon, Dad, the girls are just picking on me again!"

As kids get older, moms and dads start noticing as the children try doing some of the really important things independently. These things always seem to occur in noticeable milestones. And these milestones may be universally important but very personal. Like, when a kid is finally potty trained, or his first day in "big boy pants." How about the day the highchair gets traded in for a real chair, or the kid learns to cut his pancakes without Mom's help? Only parents can fully appreciate these moments.

One of these milestones is especially personal. That is in the arena of personal hygiene. All of my sons have had to learn to shower with Dad, so little naked butts are no new thing for me. But when it was his turn, my five-year-old Mikie provided me with the most extraordinary insight into a child's mind.

MOBY DAD I: ADVENTURES IN LIVING

When the big day came, I told Mikie he was going to take his first shower with Dad. I said he should get his stuff and meet me in the bathroom. He let out a joyful shriek and scampered away.

He showed up naked, with four turtle toys and a dinosaur.

I, on the other hand, showed up dignified, and in my underwear. Good example, I suppose, but it made no impression on him. I could see the time had arrived for some compromise.

"Okay, Mike. You can take the dinosaur into the shower, but you need clean underwear, PJs and a towel. And turtles don't need baths."

"This is a shower," he reminded me.

"Yeah, but turtles don't need showers or baths. Besides, only one toy per shower. That's the rule."

"The rule?"

"Yeah, that's right. It's the rule."

"Mom never said that."

(If you challenge Dad, you can only do it with a strong ally.)

"Well, that's 'cause it's Dad's Shower Rule, not Mom's. Anyway, you've never had a shower with Mom, have you? She only lets me take one toy."

I was trying to strike up a little humor, but he wasn't buying it.

44

"Let's ask Mom anyway." His was an impish face, wrinkled with determination.

"No. Look here, shorty, this is Dad's shower. And it's Dad's rule."

He suddenly relented.

"Oh, okay Dad," he said as he tossed the turtles onto my dresser just outside the bathroom door. "I'm ready."

"What about your towel and underwear?"

"Oh, Dad, I forgot." He hung his head.

"Well, go get 'em. I'll wait."

"Dad! I'm necked, Dad, and the girls will see me."

We just can't have that, now, can we?

"Well, grab your towel and wrap yourself up. Just be sure to bring back your underwear."

"Dad, my towel is in my bedroom. 'Member?"

"Oh, that's right. Well, use mine."

"Okay." He took the towel in hand and dragged it away. He didn't make a single attempt to wrap himself in it and gave no thought to the girls, none of whom saw him anyway. He returned to the bathroom quickly, bearing his underwear and another dinosaur. Actually, I was grateful that he had not wasted time, because his attention span (30 seconds or so, about average for a five-year-old) would not lend itself to the accomplishment of multiple tasks. But the mission was still incomplete.

"Okay, fine. Where is your towel?"

He hung his head again. "Well, I just had to get this dinosaur."

"Only one dinosaur, remember? You already have one. Now, go get your towel." Dad was losing patience.

He ran off and returned again with his towel, and without mine. But I didn't think about it at the time. The water was hot now, and I watched as he wordlessly threw the first dinosaur into the shower.

"Dad …"

"Yeah?"

He stood tentatively, with his hand stuck through the curtain, testing the water.

"Good. He says it's warm, Dad. Can I get in now?"

"What?"

"He says it's warm now."

"Who says?"

"Rex, the dinosaur. Can we get in now?"

"Yeah. Better let me go first."

I got in, and it was perfect. I realized that this wouldn't be quick, but hoped it would be educational. Little did I know.

"C'mon, Dad. Can I get in?" He spoke impatiently from outside the curtain.

"Okay, step carefully."

He dutifully tiptoed into the shower, and I closed the curtain.

"Ooooohhh". He sighed as he stood under the warm water. "Wow, Dad, this is great! Hey! Dad, get out of my water. C'mon, Dad, stand over there!"

And so it went, as Mikie hogged the first few minutes of our shower. Time for the real business.

"Get your soap."

"Wha …" He tried to turn around, but the water spray got in his eyes, and he turned back, away from the stream.

"The soap, get the soap. That's right. Skin a bunny!"

He raised his arms and I soaped him up. He made a token gesture, supposedly to scrub himself, but the move was clearly designed only to appease me so that he could get back under the stream of hot water. His so-called attempts had no hygienic intent.

"Okay, my turn." I let him have the stream and started scrubbing myself down. For the first time, he was free to look about the shower without spray in his face, and he began to do the "curious kid things." Of course, this happened about the time I had soap in my face and hair.

"Dad?"

"Humph?"

"Dad … What is that?"

"What? Just a minute … can't see. Whoa, boy!"

I got my eyes cleared up about the same time I jumped two feet. Mike was as surprised as I.

"Mikie, what are you doing?"

"Dad … what is that?"

"Well, you have one of those. What do you think it is?"

He knew, but he obviously hadn't been aware that Dad had one.

"But … Daddy … mine is little. Yours is … well … big."

"Well, Mikie, you're little … I'm big. That's all. But you can't be grabbing anyone else's, okay?"

I admit that I felt a little strained, but I really tried to keep my cool. I was taught in a parenting class that I shouldn't over-react to these awkward moments. Some things are easier to be cool about than others, I suppose.

Anyway, we had another brief review of the birds and bees. No, regardless of what Jeffrey has told you, Mom doesn't have one. The girls either. And yes, the boys, all boys, have one. And so it went.

He breathed a sigh of relief. I had answered all his questions, and he had apparently been bothered by them. But as I began to recover my washing routine, he started again.

"Dad?"

"Yeah?"

"What is this?"

I wasted no time looking, I can tell you. This time, thankfully, he was gazing at the floor of the shower, pondering something cosmic.

"What are you talking about?" I asked.

"This." He wiggled his big toe.

"Son? Your big toe?"

He looked up at me, disgustedly sputtering and stomping his foot on the shiny drain cover.

"Oh, that's the drain."

"What's a drain?"

I was busy rinsing off, and I didn't think he was serious. His cold stare brought me back to reality.

"Well, okay. That is where the water goes after it hits the floor."

"Dad?"

"Yeah?"

"What would happen if we didn't have a drain?" he asked as he placed one foot as fully over the drain as he could. That foot covered one-third of the drain.

"Well," I started, "the shower would fill up."

He promptly put his second foot onto the drain, obviously trying to cover it completely.

"How full?" he demanded rudely. Seeing it wasn't even slowing down the draining water, he knelt and placed his hands on the drain too, trying to plug the gaps his feet left.

"Real full," I said evasively, fascinated by his determined innocence.

"Could we drown?" he persisted as he finally planted his naked butt on the drain.

"It would be pretty tough, Mike. See that ledge?" He looked at the lip of the shower, then at me. "The water would have to overflow that, then fill up the whole bathroom, then maybe the bedroom—"

"Dad!"

"Yeah?

"Okay, Dad. I get it." He got up, still disgusted. "Now move over, will you? I need some of that water."

"Oh, no you don't! We have to wash hair now."

"What?" He could see that he was going to have to get it wet, so he hurriedly ran his head under the water.

"Okay, my hair is wet. Now what?"

"Well, let's get it really wet, okay?"

"Wait! Dad, do you have a washcloth?"

"What?"

"Dad." His was a pleading voice now. "Dad, I don't want my eyes wet."

"Okay." I handed him the washcloth, and he covered his eyes and walked into the stream. He tried to put his hair under the water, but only got his face wet.

"Son, turn around."

"Oh," he said sheepishly.

He still seemed not to be able to get under the water, so I pushed him gently. He shrieked and gagged.

I was startled. I looked closely to see what the problem could be. He whipped off the washcloth and stared up coldly.

"Dad! Why did you do that?" he sputtered.

"What?" I yelped.

"My ears, Dad. My ears are wet now. I hate that." The stony look he gave me made the water seem colder.

"Well, son, you have to get your hair wet to wash it. You just have to hold your breath and get under the water."

He was not convinced.

"Don't you push me again. I'll get it wet. Promise?"

I shrugged, doubting. But this time he did pretty well, and I had the soap on his head before he could blink. He struggled a bit in the rinse, but he did pretty well in the end.

So, now it was time to get out, thank Heaven.

He hopped out onto a tiny towel we use as a bath mat, and then went over and wrapped himself in his big towel. He shivered happily while I shut off the water. Then I reached out for my towel. Nothing. I looked around and then stared at him. He chuckled gleefully.

"Dad, I think your towel is in my bedroom."

"What?"

"C'mon Dad, you let me use it, didn't you?"

"Yeah, okay. Well, go get it. Hurry."

"Whoa, Dad. It's cold out there. I have to warm up first." He grinned impishly.

"Mike, do you want to go to bed early for a week?"

You have to threaten 'em where it hurts, and they can't relate to anything bigger than a week. Anyway, all "a week" means to them at this age is more than a day, which they cannot bear to think about.

"Oh, all right," he said quietly. But as I started to step out of the shower, I saw a gleam flash in his eye. He snatched up the little bath mat from the floor so I couldn't step out, and darted out of the bathroom.

"Come back here, you little …" I hollered. He giggled as he ran down the hall to his room, where I hoped his memory would last long enough to bring back my towel.

But as he ran away, I overheard a classic conversation.

"Mama! Mama! Daddy and I are going to take another shower tomorrow!"

"Oh, what fun! And just what will happen if I decide to take that shower with Dad?"

"Ha! Dad couldn't have any fun in there with you!"

The Louisville Slugger Philosophy of Life

One day in … well, I don't remember exactly when … my oldest daughter, Nicole, then age 15 years, 11 months and 28 days, came to me. In her hand, she held a legal-size yellow pad, a pencil and a determined look in her eye. She flicked off the TV. She sat down and stared at me with a new intensity.

"Well?" I asked uncertainly. After the constant nagging I did about all the TV they watch, I knew I could not show my frustration at having the darn thing shut off in the middle of the news.

"What are the rules, Dad?"

So now I knew what she wanted. I was stunned to think the day had finally arrived. She was soon to be 16. She was going to date. We made up no new rules in twenty years as our family went through life. And she was my number three. But she was my oldest girl, and maybe she felt the rules would change for her.

I reviewed the old family rules with her. All our children knew the basic Mormon rules in my house. No dating until age 16. And with very few exceptions, only double dating until age 18. And Dad wants to know where yer goin', with whom, and the ETA (estimated time of arrival) on return to my front door.

And the arrival darn well better be real close. Unless you need to come in early, and then Dad will be all smiles.

Of course, Dad meets every young man first, and gets to 'splain the rules to him. Prior to their departure we discuss destination, ETA and activities planned … and we detail the activities. I persuade the young suitor that dire consequences will be the result only of PPPP (sparing you the complete lingo, pretty poor prior planning) and that he will be well received if in full compliance with our agreement.

She picked up quickly on my desire to meet him first.

"Daddy … you won't really … well … scare him off, will you?"

Here was my young beauty, one who would make the rules and pick her winner with numerous sad losers around her. I thought to myself she was afraid I would ruin her social life. In reality, all I wanted to do was create an effective climate of consciousness that two young kids might not lose when they were alone, in a dark corner, trying to figure out the mysteries of life.

"No, baby. But I will explain yer daddy's Louisville Slugger philosophy of life to him."

"What?"

"Louisville Slugger. My Louisville Slugger philosophy of life."

"Daddy! Don't play around Dad. What does that mean?"

"Angel, I am not playin'. And I will explain it so even a moron ... er ... he will understand it. Don't worry. He can't take offense."

She was looking frustrated. She had made so much progress during this "interview" that I did not feel she could stand any serious bonehead mistake on my part. My completely insensitive candor had no place here, so I reached over and hugged her. Then I pulled her into my lap. I was on a recliner, and she sat in my lap for the last time I can remember. I knew it might be that way. She might be too grown up to share this sort of moment with me again, but it was very important for her to know my love for her.

"Angel, you don't know how much yer dad loves you. Or what he would do for you, if he had to, to ensure your happiness or safety. So listen carefully."

She had been at the brink of tears and was happy to let me hug her, so she was quiet. I started gently.

"I remember once, when you were a child and traveling with Momma and Daddy, you woke up from a dream and you were crying."

She listened quietly.

"You were so happy to feel me hug you that you smiled from ear to ear and said you wanted to live with me forever."

She giggled and hugged me back.

"I had laughed a bit, then told you that you would meet Prince Charming, and he would snatch you up and run away with you to live happily ever after."

Nicole said nothing, just listened.

"You burst into tears, saying no man would ever take you away, and that you didn't want to leave. I reached down and picked you up, held you close and told you that you would never have to leave, and you could stay as long as you wanted."

She giggled again, then snuggled a little closer.

"You slept with Mama and me the rest of the night, and in the morning, it was forgotten."

I looked at her a moment and went on.

"Well baby, I have a rule I have learned from Grandma Fancher. I will never interfere with my children in their selection of spouse or in their marriage, so long as minimum rules are obeyed."

She pulled back and looked me in the eye. I could read her mind.

"You see, all my rules will make you happy. Maybe not just now, but eventually all of them will ensure you have a chance to be really happy. That means I will do all I can to prevent you from making terrible mistakes with your life. You cannot simply run out into the world and bring home a drunk, a man who does drugs, steals or chases addictions of any kind. I will not allow it.

And after your spouse is chosen, you cannot simply get mad, leave him and come home, for example. At least, not this home. You will have to work it out. With him."

"Okay, Dad. I think I get it. What about the Slugger thing?"

"Oh yeah. See that bat over there?"

I looked toward the fireplace, and in the corner was the old bat. She looked over at it and took it in. She had known it was there but had never given it any thought. She nodded.

"That is my Louisville Slugger. I will take the young man and invite him to sit there … on the couch next to my chair… and tell him I would like to talk to him, man to man. He will sit down and worry a bit as we chit chat. Then I will tell him."

"Dad?"

"I will tell him that so long as you are out with him, he is responsible for the one of the sweetest things in my life … that I know you and your loving nature, and that I understand how all of that is all good."

She beamed a bit and then listened as I continued.

"I will tell him so long as he is good to you and so long as you feel good about him, he will be my friend. I will promise him that I am a powerful and helpful and faithful friend."

"Cool," she whispered, almost in relief.

"Then," I went on, "I will tell him so long as he is good to you, no matter how it turns out, I will always be his friend."

She was listening intently again.

"I will then tell him if he ever, ever hurts you or your children, I will be very displeased."

Nikki's furrowed forehead knit together her two eyebrows as she looked at the dark cloud in my eyes.

"And I will tell him, 'If you bring harm to my daughter or my grandchildren, I promise you that I will not kill you.'"

I paused for effect.

"And I will do it with that bat."

I have given this discussion pretty much in its entirety to all my daughters. They have chosen well. I have never had to make good that promise.

And for my daughters, this discussion has helped sort out some of the wheat from the chaff.

On the Image Beautiful

One day my son came home with a movie, one of those cute, stupid comedies aimed at the 12 through 18 crowd. I didn't like it, because I don't like anything that mocks all that is tradition, and I am too darned serious to let it go by without telling my sons about it. Anyway, suddenly on the screen appeared a naked girl in the shower.

The boys thought they knew what was coming. But I didn't blow up. I just explained that no happiness can be had from the casual disassembly of the mysteries of life. Beauty, real beauty, then can become lost in what I call the storm of lustful images and thoughts.

Kids need time to grow up, coupled with some form of structured value-building (i.e., family life and values) before they can make realistic judgments about what they want and what kind of beauty is real. And we all know even many supposed normal adults have trouble with value judgments such as these.

I have been asked a dozen times (by a dozen boys) what is wrong with looking at a naked girl (or words to that effect). Each has seemed surprised to learn there is really a practical reason for it. And it is important to a boy, more than to any man who may already be into this stuff. Because the boy can still relate to the reason.

Okay, suppose you had something you loved to eat. Really loved. Something rich and sweet. Or suppose it is something just real delicious. It can be old-fashioned strawberry shortcake with all the extras. Or a delicious T-bone steak, done to perfection and seasoned just so, with the perfect salad and … well, you get the idea.

I used to love chocolate covered cherries. I loved to bite off the top and suck out the filling. Oh, man! I used to dream I could eat a whole rack of those things. And I used to crave fruitcake. Not the store-bought stuff with the green pineapple and red-dyed grapes in it, but my grandmother's delicious, 47-fruit-and-nut, 12-lbs-in-a-shoebox fruitcake. The kind that, when it got stale, you could throw it overboard and use it as a boat anchor.

Anyway, I was away in the Marine Corps one year and ate myself sick on Christmas. Grandma had sent a delicious, 47-fruit-and-nut, 12-lbs-in-a-shoebox fruitcake. To this very day, I still like an occasional chocolate cherry, but not fruitcake. My sensory overload of that stuff was so extreme I have lost all desire and all appreciation for that wonderful, envy of the world delicious, 47-fruit-and-nut, 12-lbs-in-a-shoebox fruitcake. Yuk.

Pornography burns the senses just like that. It completely obliterates the appreciation of all the beauty that is more than skin deep. All porn destroys what I call "the fabric of family life." I refer specifically to that measure of patience, selfless love and thoughtful sharing that makes up good relationships.

Today a lot of porn is considered acceptable because it is only "R" or even "PG 13" instead of "X," but it is still porn. It still creates selfishness by fanning lust and feeding a deep burning hunger to satisfy an artificial need. It sells beauty for the lust of the moment. No long-term beauty is ever considered or honored in porn. In fact, no beauty that is not physical and cheap is ever shown in porn. Porn kills the ability to love. It kills the ability to share. It ruins the ability to be unselfish. It is all selfishness. It is not caring. It is not real. It is not sharing.

ON FAMILY LIVING

This is not simple moralizing. The things between a husband and a sweet wife are only part passion, even though that seems to be the only publicized chapter of the relationship. There are so very many other times.

There are "quiet" times, "work" times, "wash the dishes" times, "change the diaper with one hand and eat a ham sandwich with the other" times, and "the kid is out late and where the heck is he" times. The "Mother-in-Law" times can be disconcerting. "The baby is overdue" times can drive you nuts. There are the "Dad is gonna yell now and Mom is gonna tell him to shut up" times. There are "the neighbor is a jerk" times, "the dog is in the garbage" times, "the new car has a dent" times.

My favorites were the times when Dad came home from being away for more than a month, met by a frazzled wife and mother (of several) with a handshake and a "Welcome back, Partner. Yer sleepin' in the bunkhouse tonight." Well, maybe not my favorite times.

A happy family man has to be in control to live with these issues.

I believe while only half the married population is male, probably 80% of the reason for divorce is the selfish male. It is not always true, but most often it is. I believe unrealistic expectations and selfishness, fanned (if not created) by public display of the Hollywood version of the bedroom, is often the cause. In that context, no satisfaction is enough. Burdened by this problem, Dad may think the wife is pretty drab, but after awhile he will think the same of the next woman. Poisoned with porn, Dad simply cannot see real beauty.

No one can appreciate the taste of a vanilla wafer after four tablespoons of pure chocolate syrup. But healthy food and moderation make it possible to really enjoy that delicate flavor!

I believe no man can genuinely love a tender wife and be happy with his family if he is trashed out by pornography. He becomes incapable of gentle feelings, of tender moments, and of patience. He becomes selfish and is disappointed because his expectations cannot be met. This becomes anger, and it brings more selfishness. His heart is occupied by the trash he loves, leaving little room for anything else. He cannot see the real beauty in the woman he married, in the family he is responsible for.

Seeing real beauty, forever beauty, requires the whole heart, free from selfishness. This brings real happiness and cultivates real joy, kindness and patience. And the real beauty of a wife and family is much more accurately measured by the devoted husband and father than by the yardstick of the world.

On the Strength We Build From Differences

I worked once for a great company that treated me very well. They were not only good to me, but they were good also to most of their employees. They often used consultants from out of town to get us through whatever shortage of expertise we might be suffering at the moment. One of the brightest and most upright of these folks was a fellow named Steve. I liked him the minute he arrived in my office.

Steve has a wife, a kid, a budding career, a deep love of computers, and a terrific knowledge of goldfish, and he is a practicing Jew. I, on the other hand, have most all that except for the terrific knowledge of goldfish, and I am very interested in recent (last 100 years) of Jewish history. He is a tolerant genius, and I am an admirer of tolerant genius, so we communicate well. Or so I thought.

"Hey Steve, why not come home for Sunday dinner?"

It did not occur to me that Sunday would be a working day for him. But he graciously accepted and asked if he could bring something. I told him no and asked him if he were ready to stand in line for dinner, preparing him to eat with the six grocery burners at my table.

"And, oh yeah, we'll be having a roast …"

"Say, Dan?"

"Yeah?"

"Is that a pork roast?"

"Yep! Hey, Steve, you haven't tasted anything until you have tasted my wife's fatted pig!"

"Well … Dan … I don't eat pork."

I still didn't get it.

"Why not?"

The bolt of lightning struck me as he started in on the Jewish diet, and it showed on my red face. I started to apologize, and we laughed about it.

"We'll have spaghetti, okay?" Sure, it was okay, and there wasn't much else he couldn't eat. He would be there around 2:00 P.M., and he'd stand in line behind the kids.

Well, Sunday came, and all went well. Steve showed up exactly at 2:00 P.M., proper and pleasant as he always is. And as he walked in, he graciously handed me a bottle of good white wine. I was dumbstruck.

"Couldn't resist. This stuff is just great, if you cool it a bit. We should just about have time before dinner—"

He stopped mid-sentence, realizing something was amiss, and not quite knowing what it was.

"Why … thanks, Steve."

"What!" He still couldn't figure out what the problem was, and I started laughing.

"Well, Steve. We can't drink this."

"Why not?"

"Well, we're Mormons. We don't drink at all. But it was real nice of you."

Now Steve got it. He started laughing and apologizing, and I started laughing. I called my wife in, and she started laughing. We all cackled over this for several minutes, and the afternoon and evening turned out to be a good one.

ON FAMILY LIVING

Just after dinner, I got a call from a local motel in reference to room reservations for my company. The clerk there knew me, and rather than simply follow procedure, she went out of her way to contact me at home. Seemed that one of our guys was late, and could I please confirm or release those reservations? Thirty minutes later I called the woman back to fix the problem.

Steve overheard the whole conversation and realized the importance of our relationship with that motel, at least as far as it could affect our operations. He suggested that we present the bottle of wine to her from the company. I thought it was a great idea, and he did that the very same afternoon. It worked out very well.

Monday morning I got a call from the clerk, April, thanking me for her bottle of wine, glad to help, and "… just call if we can do anything for you folks!"

I wonder. What would the world be like if we had differences like this more often?

MOBY DAD I: ADVENTURES IN LIVING

Chapter 2

On Love

Unseen Bonds

My wife and I stopped in to shop a little at a store one evening. She happened to see a dress she liked. We discussed it in detail: the cost; the way it looked; the way it fit. It occurred to me that my opinion really mattered, and I was careful to put her in something she liked and that I liked, too. But it was no big deal. She went into a dressing room while I waited to see her in the new duds.

I noticed a man standing behind a half-full shopping cart about 30 feet away from the wall. He was a homely looking, farmer sort of man, and, being from farm stock myself, I barely noticed him at first. As time wore on I began, in my smug way, sizing up the gorilla before me.

He had a square jaw with a five o'clock shadow. He was about six feet tall, about 50 years old and maybe two hundred and ten pounds. He had on bib overalls, an old T-shirt, and a red ball cap tipped back on his head. He was a dull-looking old guy with steel-gray eyes set in a great stone face. Lost deep in thought, he was not moving, not even blinking, but staring at the door through which my wife had disappeared,.

There he was. He and his grocery cart. Waiting.

I was standing beside the wall in which the door was framed, so I could not see into it. But after a time I noticed that a hand in my peripheral vision poked out and waved at him. I suspected it was his wife. In a fleeting thought, I sympathized with the poor wench married to such a lug.

Since I was against that wall, I could see only him and not her. But I saw it all. I suppose she wanted him to see the clothes she was trying on. But he had no time for such petty things.

He only had eyes for her. His face softened, its features no longer granite against the world. His eyes opened wide to see clearly whatever she had to show him, and his features fairly lit up. His lips parted slightly, and he stepped forward about three or four inches. He looked her up and down, slowly, as though to refresh himself in the love he felt for her. And the most tender of smiles ever known to mankind tugged fiercely, almost futilely, at the corners of his mouth. It was a battle fought by the unseen angels who made this man glow in her presence, to make him smile. Those lips twitched, once.

He gave a faint nod of approval, and the eyes that adored her revealed themselves fully, only for a moment. Then the granite returned.

ON LOVE

I have a lot of things in my heart I don't, or maybe I can't, let out. Writing about the things I see has allowed me to see some things other men miss. I admit that at times I have been sort of self-righteous about it. I learned long ago that sweet love and a wonderful marriage cannot be judged from the outside. But I can be stupid about old lessons. My wife, mean as she is, is first to agree with that. Now suddenly, I really appreciated my marriage.

When my wife came out, I remembered who I was. I raced over and took her arm. She stared, sort of wide-eyed at me for a moment. I stumbled through the most romantic thing I could think of.

"Honey … you can't afford to leave me … and I suppose I can't afford to let you. But … aside from all that … you're okay, you know?"

We wandered playfully all over the store. I would not let her arm go. She kept telling me to stop all the mush and kept flapping that arm like a wounded duck to push me playfully away, until people must have thought we were crazy. It was a good night.

Buy your wife a flower tonight. You can still get carnations for less than two bucks. It's not the money. She will feel as though she really is the flower of your life. She is. Don't forget it.

Just pondering it will make you realize what a tough spot you'd be in without her.

Wanted: Army Wife

Love between a man and a woman is one of life's most baffling experiences. This is even more complicated if you happen to be a soldier. I have been married to a wonderful woman for 20 years—sometimes a joy, and sometimes a pain.

Do you know what I mean?

I am convinced that every good soldier needs an Army Wife. Any old wife may be okay for just anybody, but an Army Wife has peculiar qualities that enhance her patience, courage, willpower and child-rearing talents. She also possesses an irresistible desire to be with her husband wherever he is, and she is full to the brim with the ability to endure all things.

If I had known what I was looking for as a young man, I would have been more careful. But I could not have made a better choice.

Oh, it hasn't always been easy. Some days, she'll just get up and hammer on me. Big time. But she is an Army Wife, and the tough times have always been temporary.

Every good Army Wife will call the First Sergeant and pass a message for husband to stop off at the commissary and pick up another box of diapers. But if that old First Sergeant decides to tease his soldier about this mundane stuff, his Army Wife will call the lowliest private in the company and pass a message for Top to stop by and pick up a pair of pantyhose. Army Wives stick together, and they take care of their own. But they take a beating.

I mean, a good soldier stays until the mission is complete, generally doing what he loves to do, and what he does best. But the Army Wife doesn't get a break. If the kid is sick, well, Mom will handle it. Anniversary? There will be time next month … at least it seems that way to her.

Then there are the isolated tours. Hardship tours, we call them. Who's hardship? If a soldier doesn't like being alone a year, his choices are:

1. Suck it up or

2. Hit the bricks (get out of the Army).

I was never very good with bricks.

If you think about it, actually, the soldier doesn't have it so bad. Lonely nights, cold field problems, lousy chow, so what? His career is set, and he gets to play with his really big toys.

Mom … she pays. She may not see her own mom and dad or family for several years. She may have babies and/or a job, and she may have other commitments. She may not even have friends nearby. And when he gets home, she may not be happy to see the jerk until she has let him know every detail of her trials. Like me, he may spend the first night home after a long assignment away muttering something about how good that old BOQ (barracks) room looks … but she is worth it.

Yep. (Snort.) I am king in my home. I wear the pants in my family. At least I have permission to say so. Furthermore, I am the boss. At least I am when my sweet wife has nothing different to say. And my kids may fear and tremble at my approach. But they stand at attention when their mom has something to put out.

Army wife. Cold as steel, tough as leather, tender as a fresh carnation. Why?

In my case, my sweet wife was jerked into the army life and dragged away from her family by a stranger. (She says he is stranger each day.) She had to move herself alone first to join me at the Purgatory of Army Aviation (Fort Campbell, Kentucky) for her first tour. There she had to put up with lots of field duty. Next tour she moved my family to Germany. Alone, again, but dragging two babies this time, and pregnant. I don't know why she is still mine. Then she got serious and had three more babies. I wonder how there's any carnation left in her.

I have always teased my wife about being a mean woman. But in reality, she hasn't a mean bone in her whole body. She is the best. She has been a terrific lover, a world class mother, a wonderful hostess and faithful in all circumstances. The things between us cannot be distilled to a cheap discussion of sex, compatibility, or some strange alignment of the stars. She is an Army Wife.

Next time you break bread with some junior soldier trying to make a good career, alone, looking for the things that make good soldiers happy, remember. Your Army Wife will already understand. She may even explain it to him. Actually, I think there is a little sign hung up on the heart of every good soldier:

"Wanted: Army Wife. Only lion hearted, strong back with dry shoulders need apply. Adventure, travel, some drudgery. Great benefits. — Free soldier."

On Getting the Right Attitude

No one can make you feel or act a certain way. Others cannot make you happy, and they cannot make you unhappy. You may become that way, but trust me, you will be the guy with the attitude … and the consequences. And it may sound funny, but it is only a matter of convenience just how offended you can be about some little injustice.

Think about it. If your minister stepped out into traffic and you had to stop, you'd wave and smile. But if Tommy, the little jerk next door, ran out into traffic, you could really get cranked into some angry thoughts.

I was sitting in my church one Sunday, attending a conference type meeting of several local organizations. Six choirs had gathered from the local area. Nice folks, too, you know.

Now, I have an extensive background in vocal music. I love to sing and always have. Though not a professional singer, I have a real appreciation for serious singers, choirs and directors. Since my church has no paid clergy, it only follows that we have no paid choir directors. So as I was sitting there, pious in my judgmental way, I was pondering the old saying

"You get what you pay for." And I listened quietly as the wailing went on.

My second son, Donny, turned to me and brought me back to reality. "Dad, I love you."

That did it. My bubble burst, and I came back to reality. He meant it, as he always did. But because his comment was out of context with my selfish thoughts, it really registered. I was surprised for some reason.

I came out of my stupor of thought and looked around at all those I love so much. My sweet wife and the other five kids, each with a spirit as sweet as Donny's, were all listening carefully, in the right frame of mind. All of them were doing the stuff I tried to teach them to do and to be, each one of them growing in his own quiet way. Except me. I felt ashamed.

I'm usually a pretty nice guy. Just ask. But I can get off the track in my own snobby way at times. I think we all can. So once again I realized we have to work at developing the right attitude. And keeping it.

My favorite example on this topic of attitude is marriage. Specifically, one of the most intimate times of marriage: pregnancy. I never really gave it much thought when I was younger, because we always wanted more kids, and to do that, you have more pregnancies.

It didn't bother me the way my sweet wife looked when she was pregnant (well … big). I mean after all, I played a significant part in that, and I was sort of tickled about it. So I grew into the right attitude fairly easily. On the other hand, my sweet wife hated it—especially the last few months, when she would waddle around the house and moo at the grass outside, where people might see her. Other than dealing with her added sensitivity, I sort of pooh-poohed it all. When I wanted to fight, though, I would roll over and moo softly in her ear.

Well, after all our children were born and the Army sent my last orders to Korea, one of the things I did was gather up a box of pictures to take with me. Hundreds of them. And I bought three picture frames to hang in my room.

I got there and put about 12 to 18 photos into each frame—kids, wife and all. It was a group of pictures that caught the eye of every man who entered my quarters, one man even stopping to cry over some of them.

After I came back home and retired, keeping very few relics on my wall, I determined these to be my finest trophies. I hung them in our bedroom, where Gail saw them for the first time.

She came running up to me that day, having studied them up-close—flabbergasted over them.

"Did you put those pictures together?" Of course I had, and she knew it well.

"Did you ever count how many of those show me pregnant?"

I didn't believe her. So I went back and looked at them carefully. Sure enough, three out of four photos of her were with child. She demanded that I take them down, but I persuaded her that it was unintentional. I hadn't realized it, I explained, but I had picked only the prettiest pictures by virtue of her special "pregnant glow."

It was true. Anyway, she bought the whole line and smiled. And I should have let it go, but I just couldn't resist.

I mooed softly.

Then she slugged me.

Attitude. It takes a little work, but it pays big.

My Wife

When it comes to my wife, I am a lucky man. Some days luckier than others, you can imagine. I have been married to this wonderful woman for more than 20 years. In addition to the relative monetary stability I enjoy when compared to my several "happily divorced" friends, I really like her. But as I indicated earlier, this relationship has good times and bad, just like all other relationships.

I have a beautiful wife. And lest you doubt, her beauty runs more than just skin deep. She still makes my blood run hot, still takes good care of herself, remains faithful, takes wonderful care of my children, makes unbelievable meals, and has an incredible amount of talent in skills society-at-large has forgotten. But some days, she's kind of hard on the "old man."

Like a flower, when the sun can't be seen, she is ruined. If the sun hasn't come out for a few days, I can expect her to yell at me on Monday and then be mad on Tuesday because I didn't ignore what she said the day before. Why?

"Because you know how I am …"

I learned this lesson clearly when we were in the state of Washington for three years, near Seattle. One summer the sun just did not come out. Rain, rain, rain, all summer. My children remained inside, inside, inside. My poor wife stayed on the ropes all summer. Then came fall and the rainy season. I was not sure she would ever recover.

She knows, on the other hand, that I can be hard to live with once in a while myself. When I am unhappy with her and in a fighting mood, all I have to do is throw open the door and yell, in the royal voice of King Arthur: "Ho! Wench!" Then I have to duck.

Once I wrote an article about how to get "The World's Greatest In-laws," and it offended her. She felt it made light of our relationship. But it didn't, really. I love her parents, and I have no trouble eliciting that admission from her.

But when my business is showing a sentimental perspective on common things, I need to keep the things close to me in a humorous light, or I will be unable to write about them. I hope I have convinced her of that. But it took the usual two days.

I was a very young, very foolish, very immature but very lucky young man when I met the woman who would become my wife through an unusual set of circumstances. It was only by an odd chance that I happened to fall in love with her and asked her to marry me.

I had been away from her home town for several years, in the service. I was crazy about her older sister. When I came home on leave, I was sort of talked into doing little sister "a favor" and taking her to a dance.

But she wasn't the young girl I had known. Little sister had become a very beautiful young woman. I was dumbstruck. I treated her like a queen, and we had a great time. I took her home that evening without expecting much to come from it because she was so young. But the die was cast.

Anyway, the older sister dumped me, and I came home from the Marine Corps to a new appreciation of the wonderful things in my future wife. I fell in love with her when we went to the zoo and she started talking to the camels, as I recounted in Chapter 1.

It's a funny thing about my wife and me. To this day, when she puts her arms around me, the whole world disappears. She's all I can think about. And my kids can be fighting like wildcats; when she comes over and hugs me, they suddenly are happy as pigs. On the other hand, if she and I are scrapping, nothing we can do will make those kids happy … or quiet.

And while the things between us aren't put on, she still baffles me with her air of mystery. Sometimes it takes me awhile to figure out just what drives her actions.

Once, she had the nerve to say the unthinkable.

"What? Roses again?"

She didn't have that problem again for awhile, I can tell you. It took her ten years to tell me that because her parents owned a flower shop, and because every funeral caused that shop to stink of roses, she hates them. Okay. I can live with that. She loves carnations. They're cheaper anyway. Now she gets some as often as I can send them. She certainly has deserved them.

Okay. I still like her. A lot. Some days more than others, I admit it. But one thing is for sure: if it keeps getting this much better every year, my heart won't be able to take another fifty years with this woman.

On Noble Suffering; Letter to a Young Son

My Dear Mikie:

I felt overwhelmed by a deep desire to hold and hug my little boy tonight. I called you from my motel room in Tucson, Arizona, and spoke to a grumpy boy. But that's okay. I just wanted to hear your voice. Anyway, your sister Nancy was so excited about hearing from Dad that it was worth the call just to talk with her.

I called because I met a little boy today. He was just like you, except that he was sick. Really sick. Actually, I only saw a documentary on his life, but I felt as though I knew him very well. I felt as though I loved him like a son. His name was Troy, and he was small for his age. He was almost eight, and his sweet spirit and eternal smile looked exactly like yours, right down to the big brown glasses on his face. He could have passed for your brother if I weren't absolutely certain that my own headcount of your brothers and sisters was correct. He was always happy, and he had freckles on his nose. He loved ice cream and riding on Dad's shoulders. And he had a loving dad who, no doubt, was a better man than I.

Well, Mikie, do you remember when you had your accident? You were playing in the back yard and fell on that roll of fence wire. Suddenly you couldn't see out of one eye, remember? Do you remember what happened next? Mom scooped you up, and we all went to the hospital. You spent a week there, but it was a pretty good time. We all ate well, and you had all the ice cream they could bring you. And just because you didn't see out of that eye, why, that didn't slow you down for a minute. Your friends came to visit you in dozens, and you went right back to being the happy kid you always have been.

Well, Troy had a tough break when he was two years old. His mommy died of a terrible disease called Anti Immune Deficiency Syndrome (AIDS). She had gotten sick without knowing it, and so Troy was born with a good chance of getting the disease himself. After she died, he got it. But he was just like you, and it didn't even slow him down. For a while.

Because his mommy died, his dad raised him alone. Mikie, do you know how hard your mom and dad work? Well, moms or dads who raise kids without a partner work especially hard to raise kids because they are all alone. Troy's daddy had an especially tough time because the disease was so bad, he often had to quit working to take care of Troy. But they worked hard and did well together. They were very happy, except for the illness.

Troy was from Australia, and when he moved to his school, the town was wonderful. The parents were all so worried about the disease that they had a meeting with the principal. Everyone had heard about the disease, and they all expressed their concern for their children; then the principle introduced Troy's daddy. The parents all stood and gave him a standing ovation for his work in the town (as an AIDS prevention speaker) and for his work with Troy. After that, the whole school loved Troy.

At the beginning of the documentary, Troy was a normal looking kid, but he was only about half the size of his friends. After the disease took over, he became thinner and thinner. His life ran in cycles. He would be in school for a few months, and then he would get sick or have skin problems (open sores). He would have to stay home a few weeks. Then he would always bounce back and head back to school again.

Mikie, I thought the story might have a happy ending because Troy was so happy, so very good, and so sweet to all who loved him. I was sure he would get well. But, Mike, real people were in this story, and real people played the parts. People with AIDS die. Almost always. I know of only one documented case of a person with full blown AIDS lasting longer than 10 years. Troy died just after his eighth birthday in June of 1993.

Mike, whatever I teach you about right and wrong, remember that all sickness and disease can be had by even the most innocent and precious people.

Anyway, I promise you that if I ever end up in Heaven, I'm going to look around for a little bitty boy named Troy. And when I find him, I'm going to hug him. And I am going to tell him how I love him. And I am going to tell him how sorry I am that I couldn't help him have the life my Mikie had.

Teaching Consequences

"C'mon, son, slow down." Darn go-carts are dangerous.

"Why?" he demands. "I'm being good. I'm not on drugs, not drinking, not even breaking the law. What's wrong with some serious fun?"

"Because it's too fast." Can't the kid understand that? Go-carts are very dangerous.

"Why?" Ya just can't bear to let me have fun without saying something, eh? Again. As always."

"Because I said so. Now, don't do it. Okay?" Why doesn't the kid just stop? Don't they listen anymore?

"Look, Dad, it's safe. It can't do more than 35 miles per hour. I'll watch for other cars coming." This is stupid. Why must I explain everything to you these days, Dad? Old brain cells must stop working after awhile, from lack of oxygen, or exercise, or maybe an overdose of fat cells or something.

"Son, just slow down. Okay?"

The kid ponders his understanding of Dad and his old "five miles through bad weather and tough times" syndrome. Then he diffuses the problem.

"Oh, okay Dad." It is what Dad wanted to hear. Dad will be quiet now.

Well, it wasn't okay. The kid was whizzing along and hit a parked car. The impact snapped his neck. He thought his toy was fast but harmless. He was too proud to listen. He may never have been drilled on consequences or made to understand the danger.

I guess we can't tell him now, can we?

Parents, pay attention! Listen to kid logic: Old equates to used up, worn out, has-been, past the Best-If-Used-By date.

New is good.

Old is the opposite of new.

Therefore, old is not good.

Let's review some equations: Old = old hat, old time, old fashioned, old clothes. Stupid stuff is old. New = new car, new clothes, new stuff, new wave, new ideas. Cool stuff is new. New is good. Old is yuk. Dad is old. Poor Dad. I love him. But he is stupid. Dad always is, till a kid is 30.

MOBY DAD I: ADVENTURES IN LIVING

A friend in school had a big brother whom I didn't know very well. He had a buddy who owned an old Chevy pick-up.

They had built a go-cart and wanted to see if they could get up some speed on it. It was an old sandlot affair without an engine. The kid held a rope while his buddy towed him along with the truck. He tried to make a turn into his drive, hit a pole. He died at the scene.

His buddy was never the same.

In another tragic situation, Larry, a good 16-year-old kid, had been given a GTO (for his birthday, I think).

Now the GTO was Pontiac's prime muscle car in the mid-'60s. The car was hot. The weather was hot. Larry was out drinking and having a cool time with two friends, Eddie and another kid I knew.

Larry's mom and dad had been out for dinner and were heading home. The GTO passed them doing more than 110 miles per hour. It was flying over the several terraces in the road as it descended into the valley from the mesa. The officer in pursuit could not keep up with them.

There was a small dog-leg (bend) in the road near some cattle yards. At the far portion of this very minor bend was a telephone pole. The car could not negotiate the dog-leg and rolled onto its side, hitting the pole top first. The pole did not snap, and the car simply wrapped around it.

One kid was thrown free and died right away. Larry lived a few days. Eddie lived three months.

Okay, you get the idea here. I think parents need to tighten up. We need to promote the old method of parenting. It worked well once upon a time, before parents became too sophisticated to stand up to their kids. I am not talking about abuse or brutality. Just definition.

You see, I think I owe it to my kids to tell them what the limits are. Sometimes I have to stand up to the responsibility and refuse to negotiate. My children have come to understand there are moments when I cannot move. Each kid is just too important to me.

"I'm the dad. If this is your house, this is your law. I will not allow anything else."

What I mean to say is: Some consequences are so severe that I will not allow you to endure them.

Oh, I know. I was a lousy dad. A bit of a jerk, I suppose. But I got lots of practice. I struggled to raise three Eagle Scouts and three beautiful girls. Five are doing well by my definition. One has stepped outside the norms I have set but is doing well as far as the world goes.

Anyway, it worked for me. I give this a score of 83%. I consider it a passing grade … for a lousy dad.

A Small Town and "The Capture of Red Chief"

I live in North Missouri, near Gallatin. Small towns have their own flavor and no one can know the peace found here if they are not from a small town. Wait a minute … did I say peace?

Oh, yes. There, I said it. It is true. Even though everyone knows everyone else. Everyone knows who is new and who is not. Everybody knows their neighbor's business and their neighbor's dog, and we all grumble about what goes on and what is right and wrong. We are all mad at the outrageous electric bill, and we all know so and so is being pretty uppity considering we all know her.

Oh, yes. What a sweet life it is here.

Small town America has traditions unique to the rural life. We specialize in conservative values, quiet life and the pursuit of the American dream, whatever that may be to you.

Think about this. Original baseball teams were made up of dreamers who wandered around the country. They looked for any working team that would provide a shirt and let them in. They were scorned. They played hard and nearly for free, at dirt fields with grubby stands in every small town. Any kid with legs enough to make it to the field could watch from the closest seat to which he could stake a claim. It became the National Sport. But today, mere mortals cannot get into a professional game. Why, a professional game and a nose-bleed seat today will cost a family of two a minimum of $50.00 for two seats, two dogs and a beverage. If you want to punish yourself with a losing team, you skip the hotdogs and the popcorn and get soft drinks with no beer. It still costs $20.00. (As for me… I don't drink beer but I gotta have my hot dog and popcorn. A local softball game is just as entertaining and the dogs are cheap.)

Yesterday I went to a Gallatin softball game to watch my niece play in a fiercely contested game. For a measly $5.00, I sat next to a beautiful woman, had two huge polish dogs crowned with all the goodies I love, plus pop and popcorn. Only the adults quietly grumbled about the umpire, but they were reasonably polite. The kids were respectful most of the time, and we all complained about the high prices. It was awesome.

Okay, you know Gallatin. If you lived here, you would probably know me, because this town is so small and my bride has made my presence and her new marriage a matter of public display. I don't know a soul. I have tried to find someone I don't like but have been unsuccessful. Folks are just too dang friendly here.

Get this. I went to the local hardware store late in the afternoon. They were trying to go home early, and it was locked. They saw me at the door and let me in! First they tried to find a way for me to get my item free. But being unable, they sold one to me and ended up staying late for me. They served with a smile and made no money, but they have an eternal customer now. Try to get that service anywhere in Buffalo.

This town has a barber who cuts my hair the way I want it. (Don't laugh. A major disadvantage of Small Town USA is that you may not have a barber.) We have a florist who knows my name, a grocer who smiles when I come in and carries my groceries to the car. We have a hardware and lumber yard where service is the business they are serious about. And I have actually heard parents who have refused to buy their kid a cell phone. (Yep, I am one of those.)

I am not a Democrat (oops … a columnist should never declare his politics), and I have found no one else here who is exactly happy with the principle of spend, spend, spend.

I know the prosecuting attorney here who has one of my family in the pokey. The attorney actually knows my family member and his issues and is working to get him help! And I know other public servants who actually come to my house and ask for my vote.

But it's the kids that make a small town. It all goes back to the kids. I believe in kids. I believe in the Boy Scouts of America, in the pledge of allegiance, in public prayer, in Girl Scouts, in church youth organizations, and in anything that will continue to provide the bedrock of honest American youth. Oh, good kids come from other places, but the small town allows the rural ethic to be implanted in our youth. Our nation and the values it holds dear cannot survive without them. Let me share some episodes in our little culture.

This year there was a summer youth theater program that you may have missed. The play was just a little comedy. It was called "The Capture of Red Chief," a goofy, funny, silly little play with kids running and yelling and showing off. I attended it on a Saturday night with probably 50 other folks in the audience. It had nothing to do with talent or money or politics. If you saw it, or if you didn't, it was all about family.

Nonetheless, I have big problems. My neighbor has a man-eating dog the size of a coffee cup. My niece, who was paid in advance so she could attend summer camp, is dragging her feet to mow the lawn as she promised for the money. (That means someone else has to mow it. Guess who?) My car sounds like a wind-up toy, and I feel wimpy in it. The town may stop funding the (only) local swimming pool in town this summer. The Boy Scouts are trying to overcome a terrible and unfair judgment that may put them out of business. The far right has tried to capture the conservative voice of America, and sometimes I, Mr. Conservative American, can just spit about it. And someone is always griping about something I have done that I should have done better or faster or sooner.

But this is a great town. And I am very happy to be here.

If you think you can get a cheap dog with mustard and relish, pop and popcorn with a great ballgame anywhere else … for less than $5.00 … let me know where it is.

We can go together.

The Legend of the Lost Little Girl

Once upon a time, there was a wretched little girl. She was not unpopular, but she attracted the attention of some eight-, nine-, and 10-year-old tormentors. She was a little bigger than some of her fellows (not a lot bigger, but she was sensitive), and she was teased mercilessly. When she became upset, she would be seen as an easy target. Well, it was a wicked, downward spiral. Today, we might call this bullying.

Frustration became more difficult to deal with, and she started to show it. She would wake up mad, go to school afraid, and come home crying. Day after day. Week after week. Month after month. And as good as her school was (I consider it the best public school available in the local 100-mile area), the public school system did not allow for individuals.

Oh yeah, we might as well jump to light-speed and briefly discuss the public school system. Imagine, if you will, a teacher (a good teacher, one who cares, as most do) trying to "do more with less," as the politicians, the budget people, and the legal system like to coin the phrase. In the classroom there are 30 or more kids of all economic levels, each with his/her own problems. That might include Mom and Dad's divorce, big brother's drugs, or maybe even not enough to eat yesterday. Do you think when a teacher carries such a load, perhaps one kid might fall through the crack?

I know the idea sounds radical, but my wife and I determined to try home schooling. The idea is so unusual that a neighboring school-district superintendent recently tried to shut down a home-school in his town. It took a lawyer to get his attention. If certain criteria are met, home schooling is a legal, effective and viable way to teach (not baby-sit) children. This is reflected in nation-wide tests administered to homeschoolers.

But let's get back to the kid and our experience. We used to joke about Nancy. "How do you tell the difference between

Nancy and a terrorist?" You can negotiate with the terrorist! Or how about, "What is the difference between a pit bull and Nancy?" The curly hair. Do you get the picture?

We pulled our three youngest out of school and started. It was tough. My wife did it all. Develop the curriculum. Buy the books. Read the material. Draw up the plans. She had to develop the routine. She had to challenge each kid to use his natural curiosity and pursue the joy of learning. She had to encourage curiosity. She had to reward invention.

"Mom," our little terrorist said one day, "I want to build a city." She got out scissors, paint, tons of cardboard, little milk-carton boxes, and ice cream sticks. She drew the town on the flat box, then made the buildings, hung wire on little ice cream stick telephone poles. She even drew roads and a pond in town.

"Okay, Mom, I want to fly an airplane," and three days later she had a cardboard cockpit complete with instruments and controls.

"And how about Star Trek?" After another week, she and her brother were raising the shields and firing photon torpedoes from the bridge of the starship Enterprise.

Today Nancy, age 10, is up and smiling every day. She plays piano wonderfully. She handles horses skillfully, with patience. An avid writer, she is writing poetry and expressing herself very well. She is an artist, drawing beautifully and reworking anything she feels is inadequate. She is becoming gracious, confidant, caring, and loving.

She is happy.

But what do I know? I am only the dad, and dads aren't very objective. Judge for yourself.

Have you ever seen the way a psychiatrist can judge a kid by the pictures he draws? You know, the ones that show the blood and guns or the shrunken, brown trees of the inner city? I have seen them depict murder, abuse, starvation and torment of the soul.

Just take a gander at the picture of Nancy's panda bear. And ask a mother what it says about her attitude toward life.

On Understanding God ... And Parenthood

How much do we really understand about God? I mean, I know a lot of people who pretend to know all about Him. And we do have some fairly clear instructions. We are supposed to love and be kind to each other and to obey certain laws.

"Forgive each other no matter what. Don't kill. Be good. Wash your hands before supper, and all that stuff," as my little son says. For me, "all that stuff" didn't sink in until I became a parent.

The principles God employs seem too far removed from the carnal mind to be focused upon without specific noble purpose. Look around at any noble purpose you can find, and there you may find some mention of God. Without noble purpose, there isn't much mention or understanding of Him. But parenthood brings (with love for a child) purposes noble enough to help us begin to understand God.

For example, pure love that goes beyond rational bounds is one of the first requirements of God, at least as well as I understand them. Pure love in this context cannot be brought to any mind as quickly as to a parent's.

How about forgiveness? It is a principle closely tied to compassion and unconditional love. Forgiveness is not possible for anyone as quickly as for a parent. Parents can forgive a child nearly anything, a lot like Somebody Else I know. And a parent never gives up on a child. There is something eternal about that, don't you think?

Other principles, such as long-suffering and love of innocent virtue are veins of pure gold in the art of parenting, very difficult to find in any other discipline.

But patience is the toughest. A child is uniquely positioned to draw patience from a parent when nothing else in the universe could do it. I could never have learned it without the advent of six children in my life. Actually, I am still learning it. I am getting lots of practice.

It is not all roses, you know. The "joy in your posterity" promised by hopeful prophets does not imply that you will always be happy with your children. But there are great moments. Your child will make a gallant choice, and it will blind you with the rush of feeling that makes all your sacrifice a mere token payment on the real joy of it. All it takes is for some friend to come up and say, "Now that's a heck of a kid you have there."

ON LOVE

The joy associated with these moments are known to all parents but understood by very few. The greatest joy ever documented about God was the joy He felt for His Child. And His greatest anguish was over His Child. That sounds like a dad or two I have known.

I believe the qualities taught by parenthood are these: the ability to feel righteous joy and anguish; patience; pure love of innocent virtue; and the ability to forgive and endure to the end. I believe these are some of those "godly" attributes we are required to learn in this life.

But the world has forgotten its children. When asked what joys in life have made them truly happy, the answer for some parents may not even include the place of children. Today, more than half the couples in the United States who can have children choose not to. I don't think society in general can any longer relate happiness to having children or the joys they bring. As a result, I think the world is a colder place.

It is a mystery to me how far removed from the media version of the bedroom and "modern lifestyle" these joys are found, how precious they are, how hidden from the world at large, how unassociated with common perceptions of real happiness, and how unappreciated in modern cultures.

As I said, I may not fully understand God, but I have a whole house full of kids. I don't have all the answers, but the things they have taught me have made me better. Crazy, maybe, but better, for sure.

And, just so you know, Uncle Sam isn't doing so bad. I know of a nation today whose soldiers and rebels let their children starve. Even steal their food. But I have never known an American G.I. who wouldn't be happy to give up his rations to feed a hungry kid.

Chapter 3

Thoughts on Life in the Army

The Load We Bear

1989—We had to cooperate with Hanchey Army Airfield in all our training efforts. They handled our flight following, but we did not mix our training with their flight operations. We stayed clear as much as possible and were careful to comply with their direction. As the USPHT safety officer, I was responsible for a lot of stuff and went out there often. We also had practice areas in and around the airfield, and I was always around.

I was driving back from a coordination meeting there when I noticed a pilot walking along the side of the road, kicking a can, carrying a helicopter operator's manual.

I am no rocket scientist, but it was a mighty long way back to town. I am a quick study … I knew he was in trouble. And since I had a number of pilots out there, the chances were that he was one of mine.

Now, Army pilots generally have a certain air about them, and they fit a certain profile of habit and thought process. I mean, generally speaking, they wear a fancy watch, speak with a "Chuck Yeager" drawl, and they don't walk. So I had a feeling this kid was in deep, whatever his problem was, and I stopped to offer him a lift.

He was a good-looking kid, a young warrant officer, and he was very polite in an Opie Taylor sort of way, but he didn't speak. He just smiled until I asked him if he wanted a ride, then got in. He wasn't one of mine, I was certain, and he smiled until I spoke.

What's your name? He told me.

"Why are you walking?"

"Tired of waiting for the bus."

"You know, it's a long way back to town." You can figure out the rest. Anyway, I finally got around to saying I had a mean wife, six kids and a three-legged dog. There was no reaction. Nothing. Usually I can break serious ice with some of my family goings-on, but nothing came of this. I said it again and asked if he were married.

"Well … yes … well no … well sort of. I'm a widower. That means my wife is dead." He had a big smile on his face, but it was a smile of stress and pain and real suffering.

It was a hundred and ten outside, but I felt cold down to my socks.

THOUGHTS ON LIFE IN THE ARMY

"How old are you, son?"

"Twenty-six."

"Where did you come from?"

"Korea … I was there when she died."

I was stunned. I got my heart pumping again and went on to ask what happened to her.

"Oh, yeah. She was killed. Hit by a train."

At first I could not fathom what he had said. Whatever I expected, I couldn't believe it and thought he might be kidding … or maybe just wrong might be a better word. How can you kid about something like this? He still had that big smile. Yep. I had to ask.

"How?" He didn't hear me.

"And my three sons," he went on.

I was numb now; I couldn't swallow, and I listened more carefully.

"With her sister. Yep, her sister was with her … and her two …" He wasn't smiling now. I could barely hear him. There were tears stuck in him like a backward fish hook, and they just couldn't come out. Hell, I am not sure, but the tears in me felt that way.

"Her two children?"

"Yeah," he answered. "And an old man from town, we all knew him, he came out with the rescue squad. Tried to revive my son. Had a heart attack. Died on the scene."

He took a deep breath and the smile was back. He was in control again. I fired a bunch of questions. He was one of us, a soldier in anguish, and we damn well better do this right.

"What are you here for?"

"An advanced helicopter course. Apache … AH-64."

"How are you doing?"

"Not good."

"What's the problem?"

"Can't concentrate. Not sleeping much."

"Why don't you come to dinner Sunday?"

"Yeah, I'd like that."

"We have a lot of kids, if they bug you, tell me."

"Oh, they'll be okay, but do you really have a three-legged dog?"

"Yep, and he's ugly, but we love him."

"Good. I want to play with your dog."

"We can arrange it."

He didn't have a prayer. My children ran him over. The dog liked him too.

THOUGHTS ON LIFE IN THE ARMY

I called someone in the command channels. It was Major "Doc" Martin, the USPHT flight surgeon and all-around good guy. He listened. He took notes. He promised action. He left me wondering just what he could do.

Now, it happened that I was due my annual flight physical, just by chance, two days later. I entered the clinic at the appointed time and took my seat. There were lots of folks there, and some VIPs came in behind me.

I saw a lady captain (flight surgeon) step out and call me by name, and I told a colonel to go ahead, since I was in no hurry. He was grateful. He was, after all, a colonel, and obviously more important than I. I got no reward for this little courtesy except maybe a more efficient Army.

The flight surgeon finished with him, stepped out and called me again. She seemed a little put out, but I ignored it. Another colonel had come in, and I waved him ahead. He was, after all, another colonel, and obviously more important than I. I got no reward for this little courtesy except blah blah blah. I hoped. But I was getting kind of antsy. I wanted to get done and get back. When she stepped out again, I ignored all others and stepped up to her. She grabbed my arm.

"Mr. Kingsley, didn't you hear me calling you?"

I was startled at my first meeting with Captain Rhonda Cornum, who would become a hero in the first Iraq War in 1991 by her courageous endurance of crash injuries and torture. She was a hell of a man.

She sat me down and started in. She did not know I was there for my physical. She wanted to talk about my young pilot, the one I had picked up on the side of the road. She wanted to know all the details. I could not tell her enough. She was certain she could get him help, bail him out of his advanced course and still save his career.

She did not even do my flight physical. She got on the phone and spoke to the young man's commander. She stayed on the phone after I left. She contacted personnel, then Department of the Army Warrant Officer Management, Washington DC. She went out and met the kid. And she did it all that day. I have seldom seen such worthy compassion in the Army.

They gave the kid a break. He was pulled out of school, and the Army took care of him.

He came by to see me one time before he left, and he thanked me for helping. He was already better. I don't mean the pain, but he wasn't pulling the train alone anymore, and he knew it.

I learned a lot from that experience. For whatever reason my family is here, and his isn't. I am eternally grateful to have them. And whatever I might have done for that kid, it is not near as much as he did for me.

Authority

A hurricane is one of the most powerful and useless forces in nature. It is of little value to man. It is unpredictable, cannot be controlled and can only expend its force doing damage.

There is a convincing correlation to the man who refuses to recognize authority, whatever his station.

Emotions

Emotions, like the spoken word, are either your master or your slave. The man who uses reason to temper his emotions is the man looked to for guidance; he is respected and loved. The man who doesn't may well possess genius, and he may apply his knowledge well in his chosen field. **But he cannot be an effective leader.**

The Real Measure

We are so accustomed to achievement at the margin and so used to inflating the apparent value of individual performance, I think the ability to adequately measure either is often lost.

Our Special Profession

In my chosen profession as an Army pilot, the wide exposure to humanity, shared hardships and responsibilities provides a few precious friendships. As soldiers—and aviators in particular—the joy of flying often blinds us to the dangers of the business we conduct.

The death of one of these comrades who is not a friend can take the wind out of your sails. The death of a friend, however, deals a special blow to the aviator because it seems to be the only event his ego cannot cover.

It should have been me.

The Friend We Cherish

Some years ago, when I was new in an organization, I met a jerk. His name was Andy. He was sort of a clown; he wore a big, obnoxious watch that went well with his personality, and I didn't feel that he was sincere about anything in which I was interested.

You know how it is. First impressions last a long time. But finally we became close and worked together as casual but firm friends for three years.

Andy died today. Well … not exactly. He actually died some time ago, but he was not dead for me until today. I had left our Army unit (3rd Squadron, 5th Cavalry) around Christmas last year and had seen him almost last of all those I knew so well there.

Today I ran across an old acquaintance from the Cav. He is absolutely unworthy to speak this man's name, but as we were talking, he happened to casually mention that Andy had died. He elaborated a precious few details and continued the conversation oblivious to the steel band wrapping itself around my throat. I went away and cried over my loss.

It did not matter to him that a great man had passed from this earth. Perhaps the significance of it did not register to him. He could not see my mind's eye racing over a hundred, perhaps a thousand, quiet conversations I had shared with my friend. Or the jokes, or the common goals I had shared as a privileged secret.

We were good friends, Andy and I, and we shared common values. He and I had found little time to socialize, though we repeatedly spoke of doing so. At this moment, I would give anything to say we were close friends and got together often. But we loved our work; we did it well together, and I loved him as a brother.

Anyway, I called his wife. I was too late to do any real supporting, and I was unable to help. She was great, but it occurred to me that I had not been considered close enough to be notified. My heart sagged at the thought.

This man was a soldier with me, and we were both glad for our relationship. He was an achiever, spoke his mind, looked better than John Wayne and really liked the Army.

He had a beautiful wife who loved the Army as much as he did, probably because he did. He adored her and had a handful of good kids and dreams that he hoped to pursue one day. He loved living, and he had given it his best shot in every effort. He was one of those pilots with the "right stuff," and his talent was envied in the unit.

This man displayed honor, courage and integrity on an order that is seldom seen in the world today. His passing is a terrible loss to the Army. But he was my friend. And while my loss cannot be so clearly defined, I have learned a great lesson.

Sometimes in the pursuit of our careers, especially in the military, we get into the "zoom mode." We forget about the good things around us. Sometimes we need to be reminded of the priceless nature of the friendships we are all privileged to share.

As I have more thoughtfully considered this man, I can think of several other men I have known like him. Few of them have had such a tragedy, but I am grateful to have known and/ or worked with each one. This year I called a few of them just to give 'em a jolt of the ol' Christmas Spirit!

So take it from me. As you plod through this year, as you're wondering what kind of jerk it is you are working with, take time to ask about his wife, his kids and his dog. Ask him home to carve up a Sunday ham. You may be surprised how much you and the jerk have in common.

There may come a day when you'll be glad you did.

The Soldier's Motive

The driving force behind a soldier who loves his job and does it well is the illusion that:

1) He is the best there ever was.

2) He is indispensable to the organization.

We all know these things are not true.

But these noble and worthy ambitions are key to the success of every soldier and every unit.

Attitude

Positive attitude flows through an organization only if it starts from the top.

The Crowded Office

This essay was written in frustration once when my office shared a telephone line with three other offices. Constant conflict and busy lines created a very difficult situation, and I could bear it no longer when I jotted down these lines:

There are good days and bad days; I think it never quits;

There are good folks and bad folks, and folks who always quip.

There are some guys with the lights on who are never quite at work,

Who mumble endless nothings and always act the jerk.

To end this awful torment, I'll fain put up with plenty.

I'll take all there is to take until I've got my Twenty.

But when I'm clear this place and finally free to roam,

I smack the sorry dog who says, "Hey you! Get off my phone!!"

Perspective

We have reached an apex of history, a moment that may never be understood by future generations. The disintegration of the Communist block of nations may now continue until they are forgotten. It is still a concept this generation finds unimaginable, but which is true, nonetheless.

Communism may become forgotten. Incredible!

For those with a short historical memory, I shall explain that World War II ended in conflict with the Communists. They were the new enemy after the Nazis were defeated. Actually, even before the Nazis were defeated. And they were painted bigger than life by both Russian and American propaganda. We first feared, then hated them. I suppose that was the patriotic thing to do.

And of course, the Korean War came along next. It was a war against those devils—the squint-eyed little men who fought back and forth over a barren rock you couldn't give away in a cheap auction. Some of the less conservative types had a harder time buying into the propaganda surrounding the Korean War. But from my conservative and patriotic perspective, the Vietnam War really cheapened the rhetoric. I was not as proud to be in the service as I had hoped to be in those years. No one else seemed to be happy that I was there, either.

Lest you mistake my sentiment, I am not sure all those political anti-Communist nay-sayers were wrong, ill-intentioned or foolish. I am a devout anti-Communist, and I can recite abuses, tortures and stupidity of Communism in the most horrible proportions.

But I don't relate well to all that. I cannot relate to the deaths of zillions of people. I cannot relate to billions of dollars spent on the cold and the hot wars. I can relate only to fairly simple things. I relate to my world, my turf. I can relate to Danny.

Danny Hallows. My good friend. He was an old high school pal. We had made plans to travel the country in an old Sunbeam. We had dreams, but we never quite got out from under the draft to accomplish them. Do you remember the draft? The summoning of every fit young man for two years of military service? Well, for many years, all the nation's young men put their lives on hold to await the final disposition of the local draft board. Danny and I faced it down differently.

He joined the Army, and I joined the Marine Corps. He was smarter than I, and he went to flight school. He became an Army pilot. He was young and good looking. He was a rising star, and he was going to live forever.

Suddenly, he was dead. Killed in a helicopter crash, by those little Communist bastards. A brand new Warrant Officer, scared to death, brave as hell. Dead. I had always loved him as a friend, and I envied his place as a helicopter pilot and Army officer.

Someone sent me a letter. You know, one of the guys trying to keep us all glued together. I read it, got about half through it. I am not sure what happened next. I couldn't see anymore, and I was having a hard time breathing. Whatever it was I was doing—and Heaven knows I was being wimpy—I wasn't crying. Marines didn't cry in those days.

But I can still relate to that moment very clearly. And the conflict between my sorrow and the cheapened rhetoric grew in me.

Well, a lot of years and hard lessons have come and gone since then. I have even met some of those Commie individuals since those days. I have had this privilege twice, during each of the 1986 and 1989 World Helicopter Championships.

Surprise! I discovered them to be real people—people to whom I can relate. I have discovered they are not that bad, that awful, or nearly as single-minded as we ... as I ... had supposed. Why, the average Frenchman, and even some other Europeans, seem harder to get along with than any Russian I ever met.

They are not a bad looking people. They love their kids, their country, and their homes. Everyone I ever met was determined to make a good show for the Fatherland. In fact, each one of them sounded just like one of our guys that way.

The Russians have their own opinions, too, you know. They are not sure they like being around a bunch of Americans. Americans, they say, have an ego that is as obtrusive as their sickeningly sweet smell. (They think Americans stink, you see. Russians have no cheap dime-store after-shave and cologne in their world.)

THOUGHTS ON LIFE IN THE ARMY

All they can see is that Americans live in a country ridiculed for its wealth. But every American they know is looking for a way to make another buck. It is the only place on earth where a poor man can drive a very nice car to get a handout. Russians in general think this is wrong, and they feel pretty strongly about it.

How can you argue with that?

But it doesn't matter. Not now. As badly as we Americans stumble through international politics, we have won. We have beaten the adversary so severely that he has dismantled himself. The enemy has not become one of us, but his evolution will take him down his own path, and he shall arrive at his own freedom. He has no other choice.

To top it off, I was driving down the road one day in 1991 when I heard a British newswoman say that Gorbachev had beaten his coup. And Yeltsin had seized his new found popularity and created a new flag for the state of Russia.

"A particularly bold thing for him to do at this time," she said. Seems I remember his standing on a tank and calling for overthrow of the coup. I thought that took some brass all by itself.

"And the colors," she went on, "are white and blue and red. With a star, a couple of bars…"

What was that? I pondered on it again. The colors. The bars. I played it over and over in my mind. Red, white and blue. Where do you suppose he got those colors? And maybe some of those ideas? Maybe, just maybe, we have won in a more far-reaching way than I had ever imagined.

I'm still pretty simple minded. Maybe I still cannot relate properly to the big picture. But I can relate to Danny and all he gave up for me.

Thanks, buddy.

The Thing That Really Matters

There are lots of experts and innovations in all things. In spite of all the books written on How To Do It, there are a few simple words that still turn all heads and earn the guarded respect of every soldier, especially aviators:

"I was there. We did it this way."

Always Faithful

A man who is unfaithful to his wife is a liar and a thief. I believe, contrary to popular opinion, it is not likely that those traits can be channeled only into the private side of his life. Not one of us, and certainly no organization, ever received the public display of commitment he once gave to her.

A man who cannot keep faith cannot find happiness. And I question whether he can be a good soldier.

THOUGHTS ON LIFE IN THE ARMY

A Real Friend

A real friend is one who cannot spell fair-weather. He can be counted upon when the world cannot. He can look you dead in the eye with full knowledge of your past and your personality and look through the dirt to see the fruit growing there.

I have a friend like that. Dave. Not a close friend, just a faithful one. You may know him, but not as I do. You see, I did him a big favor one night in 1984, when he was the Cavalry Brigade Commander of 9th Aviation Brigade, Fort Lewis.

It was a fairly simple matter. And I didn't get killed.

That singular event was also probably more significant to me than I care to mention here, but he, the Brigade Commander, seemed personally gratified. As time went on, we developed a good professional friendship, which has continued to renew itself over the years.

During the Christmas season of 1991, my family caroled many families. It has become our Christmas tradition. As we were making our rounds on Fort Rucker, my wife suggested we carol Dave and his wife, Bobbi.

Well, you know how it is. Professionally, while on active duty, I would have felt uncomfortable because he is now a senior officer, and I would have flatly refused.

"But," my wife jabbed, "we're out of the Army now. Finished. And they may leave here one day, pick up another promotion or such, and we may not see him again."

Okay, I decided. We'll do it. I mean, it's not every day I see him, and he may not even know I am retired.

As is often the case, we were caroling with friends. I, the mean wife and our six kids with my friends, a young captain, his wife and five kids. Caravanning around Fort Rucker. I had not told my friend we knew Dave, nor that we were considering the stop.

My stop at the Commanding General's quarters, where Major General John David Robinson and his entourage were returning from a trip to Washington, was a severe breach of military etiquette. My poor young captain friend nearly had a stroke. But his lack of courage notwithstanding, I pressed on.

I was dressed warmly but informally, in country fashion, with bib overalls, flannel shirt and an old jacket. I had jumped from my car and walked up to the house as though I knew what I was doing. The ever-faithful aide (if I am any judge of nervous character) was prepared to throw himself on me as though I were a live grenade.

I announced we were here to carol the Robinsons. The aide was certain I was crazy and was prepared to kill me. Nobody carols anymore, you know. Especially for the benefit of generals.

"Just tell him its Dan Kingsley—"

… of writing fame, I was going to finish, but the aide turned immediately and said loudly into the house,

"Dan Kingsley?"

THOUGHTS ON LIFE IN THE ARMY

General Robinson came right up to me and shook my hand.

"We're here to carol you, sir. Do you mind?"

He looked exhausted. He started to apologize, saying that they had just returned from Washington. His wife was very sick, he explained, and he started to ask if we could come back, when my wife, who couldn't see what was going on and who had assembled the kids, started singing.

The kids followed her lead, and the general stopped mid-sentence. He started laughing and came out, started singing with us and then went back inside for cookies. His wife—his bride as he often calls her—came out and hugged my sweet wife. He handed out cookies to all eleven kids, who made short work of them, and it was a good time for two Army wives and two old soldiers.

We spoke briefly. Then it was over, and we left.

I think the world around us turns so fast we often lose touch with the good things. The more important our business, the more likely we are to be overcome by the worldly things.

But I am gratified to know a soldier who doesn't forget his soldiers. And the spirit of Christmas was there for me that night, in a simple gesture, without politics or ulterior motive. And I think it was there for my friend, Dave Robinson, too.

Happy Soldiers

Let a soldier or a Marine think he has to do something—go to a movie, take a vacation, change to a job coveted by his average peers, whatever—he will drag his feet, tear his hair out, holler as though he's about to die.

Give him the opportunity to show his stuff—leave his family for months at a time, work 18-hour days, inspire him to fight every associate to accomplish a mission—and you will have a happy soldier.

Personal Pride

In every military culture there are points of pride, internal traditions linking the individual to the culture and identifying him as part of the elite few entitled to this privilege.

"Garry Owen" is the greeting of United States Cavalrymen. They have a tough job; they are the eyes of the Brigade. They lead out in front of the Brigade to find and fix the enemy along the line of advance.

"Semper Fi" is the greeting of the United States Marine Corps. It is short for Semper Fidelis, always faithful. They have a tough job; they are amphibious assault specialists. They jump into neck-deep water with 80 pounds of equipment strapped to their backs and swim to shore. Then they run across an open beach under fire to attack a prepared enemy and stick him with a bayonet.

I am intimately familiar with both these traditions and the pride of their use.

I am authorized the use of both.

Esprit de Corps

My interest in the armed forces comes from my personal history. I am an ex-Marine (six years) and a retired Army Warrant Officer Aviator (17 years). This unusual background has always lent some unusual perspective to my decision-making and my career track.

I once heard a general say the winner of the battle is the guy who is there one day longer than the loser. In a classic battle along the boot in Italy (World War II), the Allies had already made plans to abandon an advance which had been stalled for a long time. They had, in fact, started withdrawing when they discovered the Germans were gone.

I attribute this victory to stronger "esprit de corps," the fighting spirit. The World Book Encyclopedia is not so romantic. They mealy mouth something about a "sense of union … common interests …"

I have concluded that line-unit "esprit de corps" is ingrained by the endurance of great trials. I have seen staff weenies (this is a private's reference to rear-echelon officers who are not really involved with the troops any more than necessary) with their extraordinary social lives go an entire career without much interaction. But let two privates share a foxhole for a few days under fire, and they often become pals for life. They may plan to visit, share their families, spend their vacations and money together, even work together after the fighting is over. I have seen it.

The glue of their lives is like the resin in the glue of a Stradivarius violin. It is that glue that gives the violin the magical sound people will pay fortunes to own and play. The glue of esprit de corps is like the nectar of life and living distilled. Yes, there are members of our society who would give fortunes to have its power, even to have it themselves. But the price is just like that of the Stradivarius. It is prohibitive.

How rare is this esprit de corps? It is tough to find esprit in a peacetime unit. It is the illusive gem every commander tries to give his organization. It is worth more than gold. It has the power to require the almost grateful giving of a soldier's life in accomplishing the mission of his unit. It is that spirit that allows each soldier to work independently and without detailed guidance to accomplish the organizational battle plan or objective.

In my experience, the Marine Corps, better than any other of the basic services, understands this principle. Their motto says it all. "Semper Fidelis" or always faithful. Pass a Marine you know, and if he says little else, he will say, "Semper Fi."

It is symbolic of the challenges you both have endured to be in the uniform, of continuing to endure the Marine drive to perfection, inspections, road marches, and pride in uniform. It goes on forever. Only combat troops, such as infantry, artillery and specialty forces in any of the services seem to practice this principle, as though the "average" soldier couldn't stand the strain. But every time we give a war, that puny "average guy" seems to kick tails all over the globe.

Congress has tried to reduce the business of soldiering to nearly a job these days. They sell it that way to recruit new soldiers, sailors, Coasties, Marines and airmen. They try to manage their pay system by that logic. But unless there is gun smoke on the horizon, it seems that Congress wipes its feet on the military's place in public life. They have done shameful things to us (the military) to save money or cut costs.

Want examples? How about the time they changed our payday to the first day of the following month and selling it as a cost-free way to change funds to the next Fiscal Year. It cost every soldier a day's pay, and don't forget it. And it cost the trust every soldier had in his unshakable payday, one of the very few sacred things a soldier celebrates regularly.

What about this? Almost every year pay raises are reduced and moved back to give the illusion that pay raises are in the bag, but we're saving money for three months or so. So much for the confidence a soldier has in his future pay. Then there are the pay raises that are reapportioned "for the good of the Army," such as the housing, uniform and specialty pays that go up instead of the base pay. For you civilians, this means that at retirement time, that "50%" or whatever percent you expect in retirement is really 30% of your regular paycheck. Yeah. It is all for good of the soldier. And we all believe it. Honest.

Congress seems to be telling our soldiers they make too much money and they don't do enough for it. Every congressman I know prances on every side to get military contracts, not for the good of the Army or because it strengthens the country, mind you, but because it pays their voters. They don't hide it. They brag about it.

Commanders, wake up.

None of this matters. Congress won't ever give you all you need, and they won't make these men soldiers. You must. Congress hasn't yet learned that a good soldier cannot stay for a career motivated by money, or he would be merely a mercenary. The only thing that will keep these kids around is pride. Make a soldier walk 50 miles, and he will moan for a week, but brag about it for a whole career. And the jerk who did it to him, the commander who walked the point—why, as soon as the blisters disappear, all of a sudden he is remembered as a "Heck of a Man."

Take a note from the Marine Corps.

You cannot pay a man enough money to put 80 pounds of equipment on his back, order him to jump out of a boat on a stormy day into neck deep (or deeper) water under murderous fire. You cannot make him swim to shore, then charge across an open beach to an enemy machine gun nest (which is trying to kill him and has killed his buddies), and make him stick those b_____s in the face with a bayonet.

But you can make him proud.

So damned proud he cannot be stopped until his buddies are safe.

Commander, make your soldier strive to succeed. Let him have nothing without earning it, let him exercise his capabilities, then stand aside. You owe it to him.

The soldier you mentor will be an inspiration to soldiers around the world.

"Oh, @%+*&! (Heckfire and Dangnation!!)"... Engine Failure in the Dark

Once, in 1984, just north of a little place called Badger Gap near Yakima, Washington, I had an engine failure. At night. I was terrified. In fact it is embarrassing to tell you just how scared a man can be and still maintain control of his bodily functions. But this is my story.

Those of you who have zero interest in flying stories may not want to read this. Just move on with yer morning coffee. But for those of you who like a good aviation tale, this story should be very entertaining.

First things first, for all you non-pilots. A basic premise of flying is that continued flight in a single engine helicopter becomes impractical without the engine. I have personal knowledge that the flight duration following engine failure is dreadfully short.

So it was that at zero dark-thirty hours, with the world around me as black as the inside of a cow, I blissfully lifted off the hill just above Badger Gap. I was intending to fly around the ridge to the firing range with the commander of Headquarters and Headquarters Troop (HHT), 3rd Squadron, 5th US Cavalry, and land at his field headquarters. Sparing you a lot of detail, he and I had recently had a major disagreement and had agreed not to fly together again.

True to the Army form for consistency, on this particular morning, 19 October 1984, that commander came out of the darkness and climbed into my aircraft as my passenger. Less than 24 hours since our … well, agreement … we were to become partners in a life and death struggle. We were, after all, still professionals. And like pouting children, we tried to ignore each other. He said nothing, and I said very little.

Now, I had cranked up the aircraft early because I wanted to warm it up for the passenger. I had expected the morning to be cold. It had been running for about 30 minutes and I was confident it was running well. We pulled off the hill, if I remember correctly, at about 0430 hours. That is, in the very early, very dark AM. After take-off, we gained a bit of altitude and just cleared the hill tops when I noticed the torque meter vibrating oddly.

I understood some of the gravity of it, and I began an immediate left bank to return to the hill top for landing. I realized the engine was becoming erratic, but I was not prepared for the sudden issues that developed. Suddenly the torque meter fell to zero. Barring a miracle, this meant the engine was not working. By my calculation, we were about to land, one way or the other.

I distinctly remember that needle hitting the little peg at the bottom of the torque meter. It was an eerie observation. I remember thinking, Oh God ... I don't wanna be here, and I thought I was having an out of body experience. I remember watching myself being so scared that I wanted to pee very badly, throw down the controls and yell, "Wake up now!" (This is not so funny to anyone who experiences it, I can tell you.) It was like watching a very scary movie, knowing it was a nightmare unfolding.

I leveled the aircraft and pushed down hard on the collective to begin our immediate descent. It was the instinct of years of training. The lowering of the collective was specifically to preserve rotor speed, so in the event we got to the ground in one piece, we might still make a safe landing.

I made with the John Wayne broadcast, "Mayday! Mayday! Mayday!" and gave my call sign. I discovered later the radio operator back at the unit did not understand a word I said. He heard someone shrieking but could not make out the message.

I had heard somewhere that it gets awful quiet when the engine in a helicopter stops. But that is not true. There was so much rotor and wind noise, in fact, that I had no feeling the engine was out except for the darn, very bright, Engine Out light in the middle of the dash, and that infernal torque meter set to eternal zero. Of course, the sudden beginning of descent left my stomach in my throat, so I knew my copilot was also busy checking his diminishing options. But my cross-check of the remaining instruments showed no life in the power plant. We were going to land, and soon.

Only years of training enabled me to put down my collective… because it is the control that gives lift to the rotor blades. I was almost too dang scared to lower it because I would descend into the blackness, and there were hills down there, the kind that are real ugly and are not moved by an errant helicopter. In the end, I was too dang scared not to lower it. Since I was fairly certain the engine was out, the main rotor would not keep turning if I did not put down the collective. This was to be my very first "night-hawk" (i.e., blacker 'n the inside of a well-digger's … well … whatever it is a well-digger has) autorotation operations, and it just had to keep turning.

The maneuver of landing a helicopter without an engine is called an autorotation. The trick in any autorotation is to trade airspeed for lift, so that your airspeed is very slow and your descent also very reduced at the moment you touch down. If you land it upright and intact, it is called a win. There are all sorts of names for it if you prang it in.

As I pressed the collective all the way to the floor, I yelled, "Engine out!" for the benefit of my copilot. We sank like a stone into that black valley. It got all my copilot's attention.

He yelled, "What the …"

THOUGHTS ON LIFE IN THE ARMY

Oh, did I mention there was not much love lost between us? During our entire emergency, we never used the intercom. We were too scared. We just yelled. Back and forth under out helmets we yelled all of our … discussion. It did not occur to either of us to use the intercom until we landed.

I had removed the copilot cyclic, but there was a collective at each pilot station. I noticed the throttle on the collective in my hand was moving of its own free will, and I suddenly realized the copilot was testing the throttle on his side of the aircraft to see if I had somehow rolled it off. In fact, he nearly sprained his wrist trying to move it, my grip was so tight. I suppose he had to do it. But for a second, it made me furious to have him doubt my pilot skills.

Well, it was dark. It turns out that I began my deceleration to lose airspeed and reduce rate of descent when I felt I was supposed to, but I did it firmly, so steeply and so suddenly that it startled my copilot.

So, there we were. I was scared. He was scared. I held the deceleration until the little black things (brush) on the slope got big enough to see. Well, you could sort of make it out.

I leveled the aircraft and started applying the collective. This is tricky. By now I had used up most of the forward airspeed to slow down my descent, and I had to time the bottom perfectly. I simply did not know where the bottom was, exactly. I pulled it smoothly but firmly all the way up, until I hit the stops. I remember feeling the aircraft shudder badly, indicating very low rotor speed (revolutions per minute). I instinctively gave it a second tug at the stops. I was scared to death that somehow the ground was just not there yet, and my mind was racing through all the vanishing options when we hit.

We hit hard once, then we hit again. My copilot and I grunted heavily the way a football player does when he is hit. I was sure the aircraft was damaged, but I did not care. I was dazed. My copilot lowered the collective, which I had held frozen at its highest point. But by now, I wasn't just scared. I was paralyzed.

My mind felt broiled when I heard his voice on the radio. He was calmly telling the world we were okay. All I wanted to do was scream, "What the hell do you mean we are okay? We will never be okay again! Never!"

But I held it back in my throat because I was too busy being cool. Cool is the instinct of aviators. It is the denial of reality. It is the absolute last thing you abandon before visible panic. It allows you to function in some manner until the emergency is terminated, for good or evil. But I was quivering, for cryin' out loud. I wanted to pee now, real bad. I wanted to cry. I was going to be cool if it killed me, and I tried so very hard to be cool, too. But my stress was so great I just did not know quite how to manage it.

I stumbled out of the aircraft and wrote something obscene in the log book. I could hardly read it that night. But I noted that there was an unusually high engine temperature since the engine was not running. That note would mean something later.

I was still trying to maintain control of my senses. I was numb, barely able to understand my copilot speaking to me. I decided to leave the aircraft and take all the critical stuff with me.

I took an MRE (combat ration, Meal Ready to Eat) and my operator's manual, since they were hard to get. It was 70 degrees out, but I was shaking, cold. I was exhausted. I walked away to one of B Troop's tents and started to fix my meal. I suddenly realized I had left unsecured my pistol, my gas mask, my survival radio and equipment, the aircraft key and all other really important stuff—stuff the loss of which could bring court-martial or for which I might have to pay. That's when it finally occurred to me that my brain was really fried. After my meal, I retrieved my stuff and walked uphill about 500 yards to my own tent, where I remained the rest of the day.

I baked in that tent through the heat of the day for more than eight hours. I was alone. I felt abandoned.

So... my helicopter was broken on the side of the hill below my tent. Was it my fault? I am an accident investigator, and I worried about so many things. I stewed over every minute of my day. How badly had we damaged the aircraft? Was it my fault? That is, did I miss something on the pre-flight? Did I land it properly? Did I screw up a procedure? I could not remember that I had taken a fuel sample the night before and had to go back to the take-off area and confirm it. Heck, maybe I did roll off that throttle, and maybe my copilot was waiting down the hill, just like a spider to devour my career by exposing some dreadful error.

Then disaster. During the mid-afternoon I heard my aircraft start up. I heard it run awhile from idle to full RPM (revolutions per minute) and back to idle for over an hour. Then it flew away.

I'm cooked.

I could not believe it had happened. It was a nightmare unfolding. I even ran to the edge of the hill to look down and see if I had mistaken another aircraft for my own. But as it flew off, I watched my career evaporate. I had screwed up, and someone else just flew it away.

An hour later, a lone jeep pulled up.

"The commander wants to see you."

A grimy, field-dusty sergeant announced my summons wearily, it making no difference to him if I lived or died. I dutifully climbed in, and he drove me for more than an hour to the place I had intended to fly in minutes that morning.

I stepped slowly out of the jeep at the tent where there were two dozen pilots gathered inside for a meeting. I was sure it was to be an inquisition. My maintenance pilot, CW2 Vint Fantin, stepped out and spied me crawling out of the jeep. He ran over and stuck out his hand to me.

"Way to go, Dan!"

I thought he was kidding. I was ready to deck him. This clown was always the funny man. I reared back, and at first, he thought I was kidding.

"No, no, Dan. Really! Great job!"

I took his hand, barely containing the frustration and confusion I felt. I was unable to speak. I swallowed hard and could not spit. I wanted to know, but I was afraid he was still fooling with me. He went on.

"Well, it was nothing. I ran it up, and while I was trying to figure it out, the crew chief found a loose bleed-air (pressure) line and the engine died."

"What?"

"Yeah. Really. Remember that write up about the 200 degrees? (EGT, engine temperature, which I had noted was high when we landed.)

"What?"

"Well, you wrote it up. That gave me the idea maybe you still had a fire. The engine was still running, but slower than idle speed."

"What?"

I could not hear him, or at least understand him. I could not see him because my eyes were full of tears, and I was still trying real hard to be cool. Couldn't let him see this.

"Really. When the TI (technical inspector) touched the fuel governor, it quit. The connector, factory torqued, was loose and the engine rolled back to flight idle. That's all."

"What?"

"Yeah. Y'oughta be gettin' a Broken Wing for that. The brigade commander is really glad you didn't break it. Anyway, the commander says it is a shoe-in."

"Broken Wing?"

"Kingsley! Snap out of it! Earth to Dan. Come in, Dan." He pretended to slap me on the cheeks.

"Vint. Damn it!"

Vint cracked a huge smile and put his arm around my shoulders.

"Dan, sit down a bit. You look terrible."

He laughed the laugh of a happy friend. I could tell he was not looking too closely at me. It was too embarrassing to see emotions this close. He was glad I had made it.

"Vint. I thought maybe I had done something wrong."

"Who told you that? We briefed the brigade commander this morning. It is okay. Yer a hero."

One by one, all the pilots in the tent did the "homage thing" and dutifully shook my hand. Two weeks later, I did get that Broken Wing in front of a gazillion pilots gathered in the time-honored tradition of the "aviator gawk," or "let us all gather 'round and envy him."

THOUGHTS ON LIFE IN THE ARMY

As I stood in front of that assembly, no one knew how cowardly I felt. Or how scared I had been. Or how unworthy.

But I knew the truth. Vint, he knew the truth as he tried to laugh with me after the accident. A few others at that assembly, they knew it, too. If I had crashed and rolled down that hill, my fault or not, I would have been poor … poor … dumb Dan, not the hero. One little moment of good luck breathed new life into my career. But many of those guys bought the brave, bold, competent aviator image. Many still do. But regardless of my personal feelings, I accepted that award.

Now I will reveal to you that there is a little private secret among Army aviators. A Broken Wing is not actually an Army medal. That is, it does not indicate a job (such as infantry, or aviator). It does not indicate a hazardous duty (such as submariner, or parachutist). It is a badge of honor, a tiny little half wing, awarded by the U.S. Army Safety Center with a certificate that says yer a heck of a man.

That tiny trinket is recognized and coveted by all Army aviators because it implies great skill performed under life-threatening pressure. It is an unofficial award for safely bringing an aircraft and crew home in spite of the odds. And all Army aviators know it well.

The chain of command quietly allows you to pin that tiny medal to the back of your cap, in spite of a strict rule against unauthorized additions to your uniform. It is a nearly invisible, hardly noticeable token of the monster aviator ego. But every soldier with wings on his chest can tell you who, around his unit, has one. If anyone does, indeed, have one. And you cannot even buy one, as I discovered when mine was stolen. Only the safety center has them. But because I am an old retiree, they have allowed me a replacement.

I know better than to fall for that old ego stuff. Life is just a little sweeter now. Air tastes better. I am just a man, and I do what I can. I am not a hero, but a lucky imposter. And I know now whatever I do, if I can feel good about myself, it is enough.

I have been retired 20 years, and I still wear the damn pin on the back of my cap.

I just can't help myself.

Work Order Heaven

For every bit of Army work, and for every project planned, every repair, and every effort expended, the Army requires a work order. It is a form (including four copies) that is inextricably linked to anything required in the Army.

This pathetic poem is dedicated to every Army Aviation Maintenance Officer, Motor Officer and accountable hand-receipt holder in the Army. Not many soldiers truly understand

THOUGHTS ON LIFE IN THE ARMY

the Army Work Order Program. But this may spark a (not-so-happy) memory for all us old retired types.

When you think of the best we always request to make our missions go well,

And the quality stuff we buy in the rough to make our field-life swell,

It's tough to explain why a mission goes bad when you worked so hard to break even.

But it's the Work Orders you submit--they catch cold, they get sick.

They die and go to Work Order Heaven.

Now, you never can tell the things that will swell in the head of a miserable supply clerk.

And the things that can fail when he sits on his pail, determined to get even with some jerk.

And no respect is given to that private, who is livin' in the supply shed behind headquarters.

But his hand and his deed will determine the speed with which you will see your next Work Order.

Make him mad, make him sad, embarrass the lad, and get the last laugh for the moment.

Put the bad mouth on him, but then watch him grin, and take your Work Order and hold it.

MOBY DAD I: ADVENTURES IN LIVING

He says "I don't take revenge, don't hold a grudge, and I certainly don't want to get even."

But when he shows that fat grin, you know it'll be him, when it all goes to Work Order Heaven.

Work Order, Work Order, where have you gone? You were ready but now what's amiss?

The last you were seen, the supply clerk had screamed, and then he gave you a kiss.

The Work Order went out, we pulled strings, used our clout, and delivered it tidy and ready.

All papers prepared, documentation well fared, then the supply sergeant took it to study.

But the next day was bad, we knew we'd been had, and the commander was beginning to wince.

He had tried the initiative to seize, the Big Boss to please, but had missed the Work Order suspense.

Now, Ehrhardt's still missing, and Hoffa's under the stadium. Has your Work Order suffered this fuss?

But that ridiculous trivia can do nothing to rattle ya like this "missing Work Order" stuff.

So the ulcers are flying for the men who are trying to keep that Work Order afloat;

THOUGHTS ON LIFE IN THE ARMY

But it's the clerk who is laughing at the commander who is crashing, and the clerk who has time to gloat.

Remember, my friend, this tale has its end in the Work-Order success we all covet.

But the key we can see is not you, and not me, but the Work Order clerk who can cut it.

So do your papers aright, dot your i's, stop this blight, and don't let the clerk get even.

And we'll make justice alight, close the breach, win the fight. And keep all this stuff from Work Order Heaven.

MOBY DAD I: ADVENTURES IN LIVING

Chapter 4

Holidays

Dear Dady

While I was in the Army, I served a very short "isolated tour" (only seemed like two lifetimes) in Korea. I quickly learned there was a lot of difference between being alone and being away. Many soldiers, even the married ones, were alone. We all knew it was part of the game if you wanted to be in the Army. But although you almost never heard from anyone having problems at home, it was a hard time.

I suffered without my family. My sweet wife mailed old and new family pictures regularly for me to rotate through a few old picture frames I kept. Men would often comment on my display of family, kept on a special wall visible from all parts of my room. Once a man visiting me for some reason stopped mid-sentence, walked over to my display, and asked me about them. As he listened, he began weeping. We became fast friends.

MOBY DAD I: ADVENTURES IN LIVING

When I arrived in Korea I was very fortunate to be sent to a little unit that had a small version of every imaginable facility on the compound. It had a little library, a fully stocked commissary, a PX, a small gymnasium, a theater, a little restaurant and an officer's club. And the little town off-post was friendly, so I was very happy to be there, as long as I had to be in Korea.

As soon as I signed in, I went to the post library. I discovered it was not only well stocked, but it also had a program that allowed us to borrow books from all American Army libraries in Korea.

I had a burning desire to be close to my children, so I began to read children's books on mini-cassette tapes and send them home. I soon went through all the children's books the library had. I drove the librarians nuts by asking them to go through the lending system around Korea to get more.

My youngest three children were thrilled.

I did some pretty clever things. For example, as I was speaking to the kids, I would say… "Now, don't tell your mom these things, but … gab, gab, gab."

That was just a three-alarm fire to them. They would leap out of bed, holler for their mom as loud as they could, and make her sit down and listen to all the dirt. It was cute the first dozen times, but after that, she got pretty tired of it, especially since they did it for nearly every tape.

HOLIDAYS

Of course, the kids had favorite tapes, ones Mom got tired of hearing. Then there were Mom's tapes, to which they would sneak in and listen closely. But the fact that they had received so many really bugged my poor wife. She would, in a bad moment, ponder the lot of a woman alone with six kids and feel cheated of my time … and maybe even of my affection.

One day, after having blasted me with the only real problem she would admit to having during my whole tour (she did wonderfully well), she yelled that this week she had received only one letter, while the kids had received two tapes. Two! And it had better stop … or words to that effect.

Well, the moment went by as bad ones do; she was sorry, I was sorry, and soon it was forgotten … until just before Thanksgiving Day. Opening my mail from home, I among the other contents a little, triangular letter. It was all folded and taped up so no one could read it before its intended addressee. In it, I got this heart-full from my seven-year-old daughter, Elizabeth:

Dear Dady,

I heard mom talking to you on the telephone. She said that you should not send the little kids any more tapes with storys. Dad the little kids love those storys. You just can't stop sending us little kids tapes with storys on them. She said you don't half to read storys you only need to read one page of a story. Dad please understand. Please write back.

Love Beth.

I was very lonely in a foreign country. Her tender heart nearly burst on the page. I broke down and cried over this sweet letter, and I immediately wrote back.

My Dear Daughter,

I received your wonderful letter today. I am so very happy to have the love of such a good daughter. You only heard part of Mama's talk, however. She told me how good you have been, and how she could not make it without all your wonderful help. She made me very proud of you.

Tell the kids I will always love you, and I will send you more tapes. I will just have to send more to Mom. Okay? I love you!

Daddy

At Thanksgiving I often ponder the many things like this my family has brought me. I am the luckiest man alive. This holiday season, I hope you may have as much to be thankful for as I.

Oh, Let Us Be Thankful

Dad woke this morning, crabby as usual. His seven-year-old daughter (Kid Number 5) appeared at the bedside around the 5 A.M. time-frame and tried to sneak under the covers. Dad tried to be furious, but she just giggled and said she just wanted to say, "I love you!"

"No! It's too early. You can't turn on the TV yet. And don't wake your mama!"

"Okay, Dad." she whispered. "I'll come back later."

It was the day before Thanksgiving. Mom had made it an unwritten family law that almost anything loving is okay, especially over a holiday. It is a peculiar law, more easily lived than explained, but the family seemed to enjoy it. However, sleeping till six-thirty happens so seldom that Mom and Dad always try to demand the privilege when it is possible.

Anyway, Dad rolled over and saw that Mama was still out cold. He went back to sleep.

Ten minutes later, along came Michael (Kid Number 6). Mikie carefully squeezed in with Mom, and Dad heard his sweet wife gasp and exclaim," Ooooh! You're cold as a pickle! Frozen! Darn kid! Can't you ever keep a blanket on?"

She curled up around the boy as he shivered happily. He savored the warmth but was silent only a moment before the boredom won him over.

"Mom," he whispered. "Is this Thanksgiving? Do we have to go to school today?"

"Shhhh, you little popsicle! Don't wake Daddy. Go back to sleep. It's too early for TV."

"Mom!" he whispered insistently. "Do I have school today?"

"No! Now! Go to sleep!" Her whisper bordered on frantic, and he realized how near he was to serious retribution. He settled down.

The clock was rounding the corner on five-thirty when Nancy crept back into the room, and Dad realized he had to make his move or lose his spot next to Mom for the day. He rolled over and caught hold of her just as Beth (Kid Number 4) darted in and dove to claim that place.

"Ha!" Dad gloated as Beth landed on a well-timed hip and rolled off. She snickered and settled for a place next to the wall.

That's when Dad lost control.

Mikie, having got loose from his mama, began burrowing his way under the covers to the foot of the bed, hoping to surface between Mom and Dad. His plot was foiled with Dad's well-placed knee, but he salvaged his mischief when he started tickling Dad's foot.

Dad hated this particular maneuver, as always. Dad would forbid this when he could maintain the "stern" face. But this was not to be one of those days. Dad started to jerk uncontrollably as Mikie shrieked with glee.

Nikki (Kid Number 3) jumped in and started doing some serious tickling of her own! Dad had just gotten hold of two children, one under each arm. Covers were flying, pillows going every which way, when somewhere in the melee Mom made her escape. She left Dad to fight off the heathen little devils alone!

"That's it!" Dad roared. "I'm hitting the shower!"

As I made good my escape and darted to the bathroom, I surveyed the scene. Donny (Kid Number 2) had joined in, and before I surrendered the bed, five kids were writhing and shrieking among the covers. My sleep was ruined, the bed destroyed. I wouldn't be able to get next to Mom until the kids were in bed that night. My boss, Mr. Scrooge, was waiting at work to tell me I'd have to make a Thanksgiving Day appearance.

But I wouldn't trade any of it for anything I can think of. And when you think of kids or marriage as sacrifice, remember that the return is exactly one million times what you may put into it.

And give thanks.

Christmas Traditions Are Made Of These

'Twas a few days before December, and Thanksgiving was still fresh in our memory. It had been a wonderful time. Friends had jammed into our tiny kitchen with the smell of cakes, pies, turkey and all the ice cream our six kids could pack in. I had been out working early on this morning. Our 14-acre place was demanding some attention during my off time.

I pulled into our yard with my little pickup and backed up to the barn with a load of feed. The door burst open wide, and my four-year-old daughter came squealing out from our double-wide mobile home. She wore no jacket, boots untied, the voice of her mother following closely behind, "… and shut that door!"

Nancy didn't pay any attention.

"Daddy! Daddy!" She was beaming, her little round face flushed in the brisk morning air. I stopped what I was doing and pointed toward the house.

"Jacket!" I said firmly. "Go on!"

She pulled up her run, and the wide smile vanished. She frowned, turned slowly and trudged back into the kitchen. In a moment she came howling back out the door, jacket barely on one arm, boots still untied, and the voice of her mother following close behind.

"… and shut that door!"

Bang!

She slammed the door and scampered the distance between us like an Olympic champion. She arrived before me, runny nose, hair disheveled, barely dressed.

I laughed inside to look at her, radiant in her joy to be near her daddy. She had an urgent message that would cause her to bust if she didn't get it out! But it was cold, so I set my sack down on the truck and looked at her as sternly as I possibly could. It wasn't very effective.

"C'mon, munchkin. We gotta do better'n that."

I knelt and tied her shoes while she got her breath.

144

"Daddy!" she whispered breathlessly. "It's Christmas in there! Mama has all kinds of lights up! And Christmas stuff!"

Her face nearly burst with that broad smile as I buttoned her coat. She seized my ears and pulled my face down for a sloppy kiss right on the mouth. Her nose was runny and her hands were frozen, but it didn't seem to matter, as long as she was with Daddy. I couldn't help but laugh again as I wiped my face.

"Okay, pretty-girl-of-my-life, later we'll go in for lunch and you can show me. But right now I have a lot of work to do."

"No, Dad! C'mon Dad!" She had my arm and was trying to get me in tow. Just a little momentum, and she was sure she would have me.

"Nancy! Now, you know what there is to do."

She suddenly relented, and I could see the little wheels turning.

"Okay, Dad. Say, I'll help you! I'm your helper, right?"

I tried, but she must have noticed that I didn't show quite the enthusiasm I should have. She paused for a response. Then she coaxed me.

"Right, Dad? Huh. Isn't that so?"

I am not sure how you other dads handle this sort of thing, but I am a wimp. I know a four-year-old girl has a limited number of things she can do with a 50-pound sack of grain, but I just didn't have it in me to tell her. I spied a rake and hit on a great diversion.

"Say, honey, why don't you take this rake and gather up some pine straw for Joey [the pig]?" I offered hopefully.

She took the bait. "Yeah. Yeah! Dad, I'll get that!" She grabbed the rake and ran off excitedly.

It lasted for one sack of feed.

When I returned to the truck for my next sack, she was waiting for me with her arms folded and a look of sheer disgust on her face.

"Oh, Dad," she said, sighing. "I want to help. I am a big girl now. And I want to carry one of those sacks!" Her once-folded arms were now held out expectantly with a funny little Don't pull one of those tricks again, buster looks on her face. I was trapped.

"Sunshine, you don't understand. These things are heavy."

Another look of disgust. I began to crack under the pressure. Hands still out, she was still waiting for the expected sack of feed. Another moment of waiting, and those little hands began to open and close impatiently. I couldn't stand it anymore. Discipline be darned; I caved in.

"Okay, but I'm telling you, these things are heavy!" She giggled and the look of pure disdain changed to one of those Okay, schmuck, give it here! looks.

I reached into the truck and pulled out a sack. I looked at her doubtfully. She stepped forward defiantly, as though reading my mind. She was determined not to let me chicken out. I swung it off my shoulder and held it in my arms. She stepped forward and placed her arms around it, then started backing away.

"Okay, Dad. I …" she hesitated, then groaned as the size of it finally registered, and the weight of it finally seemed to ring a bell. "… got it."

She tried to back away as I slowly eased it into her arms. Her face began to show serious effort as more and more of the real weight became her burden. She started to sag as I lowered it, first not being able to stand quite upright, then bending slightly, and then trying to balance the weight of it on her knees.

Finally, she had the whole thing, sort of draped across her bent knees, head reared back, tugging with all her might to stay upright, tendons showing in her tiny neck, with nary a whimper.

At last, through clenched teeth, eyes slammed shut and straining with all her might, she groaned.

"Okay, Dad, you can help me with this one."

I lifted the sack and returned it to its proper place on my shoulder. Nancy straightened up with all the dignity she could muster and began to brush herself off.

"Whew! Dad … those things are … heavy!"

She scrambled into the back of the truck as I told her the sack weighed more than she did. She was not impressed.

"Dad, I weigh forty. Forty, Dad." Disbelief weighed her face with a frown.

"Honey, this weighs fifty pounds. That's more than forty pounds." I watched as the light came on in her eyes.

"Wow! Dad, that's a lot! I'm strong! Look here, Dad!"

I turned around to see her standing among the sacks of feed, coat off now, arm bent in the classic Arm and Hammer pose, massaging her bicep as though she were able to make it grow. When nothing happened she noticed I was watching, and in a nearly desperate effort, she said again, "Dad! Look here, Dad!"

Now she tightened the bend in her arm and twisted her wrist first inside, then outside, and proclaimed, "See that?"

I strained to see so much as a ripple of hope in that muscle but failed. I mumbled something conciliatory.

"Told ya! Yeah, Dad. I'm strong!" She sighed deeply and looked around at her kingdom. She was about to become bored again, and I could tell that only a miracle would deliver her from more mischief.

"Well, think I need to help Mom now."

What a break. I was relieved.

"Oh, what a good idea, Nancy. You know, not all girls are as helpful as you are."

Her face lit up, and she glowed in this new praise. She turned abruptly and ran into the house.

I went on to finish several other chores that afternoon. I was about to repair a broken water pipe when Nancy ran out again. Her shoes were still untied, her jacket unbuttoned, and as she sped out to the barn, the voice of her mother again followed closely behind, "… and shut that door!"

Bang! The door shut loudly, and she ran out to be with her daddy again.

I laughed and set my tools down. Then I went through the drill of getting her fit for the outdoors again.

Her little face furrowed. "Dad, whatcha laughin' at?"

"Oh, I was just thinkin' about all the sacks you can move for me."

"C'mon, Dad. I know yer not. What's so funny?"

I could not find the words to tell her how much I loved her at this moment, and I knew she would not understand. So I did the diversion thing again.

"Oh. Well, I thought you were in helping your Mom."

"Oh … that. Well, Mom is … er … I guess I am done helping Mom. I'm helping you now!"

She looked up, hoping not to be sent away, obviously needing to be wanted. I was smiling at her, sort of rejoicing at this little bundle of pure joy, grateful that I could have a child with such depth of feeling. At this moment I was keenly aware of the sweet woman who made her this way. My smile seemed to feed that bursting grin of Nancy's again!

Suddenly the smile faded.

"Dad?"

"Nancy?"

"Dad, yer supposed to say 'What?' So, say that when I say 'Dad?' Okay?"

"Okay, Nancy, now what?"

She drew a long, nervous breath.

"Well, Dad … ya know the animals and the Baby Jesus?" She was referring to the beautiful manger set given to our family by friends when we left Germany.

"Yes. What about them?"

She drew another long breath. "Well … Mikie broke the donkey. He did it, Dad."

I tried to be upset, but I couldn't muster it.

"Okay. We'll try to fix it when I get in for lunch. How's that?"

"Dad!" She was furious. "Mikie lost the leg! Mikie!"

Take your cue Dad. Get mad, she seemed to say. But I just couldn't do it.

"It's okay, honey. We'll find a way to fix it."

Well, that was several years ago. Nancy is all grown up now—eight years old—and she has finally admitted that Mikie didn't really break the donkey.

But to this day, the Christmas season can't get started at my house until Nancy and I find a way to prop up that three-

legged donkey on our piano … with the other animals, and the
Baby Jesus.

"Daddy! A man called"

My daughter, Elizabeth, is 18 years old and full of life and
happy stuff. She has been the joy of my life, and I readily admit
that my smile these days is very often over her pranks.

I came home one night recently, full of the doldrums that
the working world gives you. I was determined to go down
to the store, blow a wad of money ($4.00) and pick up some
cheap pop. I asked her along, and she jumped at the chance.
She immediately demanded to know where we were going.
Then she had to know what I was buying. And she fairly coo'd
over the three liters-for-two-bucks deal.

We got there, and she started picking it out. I told her to
cool her jets, I was buying so I was choosing. She slinked
along behind and started harassing me.

"This one has caffeine … no one likes that one …" and I
tried to run her over with the shopping cart. She giggled, stole
my cart and started riding it up and down the aisle while I made
my selection. She looked like she had lost her mind.

"Dad! Look! This is the shopping cart ballet!"

When we went outside, she lost it. She stood on the back
of the cart with her arms outstretched and zoomed past me.
Then she did it on one leg, then on the other. Then as she
passed me a fourth time she held her arms in a circle above her

head and declared it to be a ballet move I cannot spell. I am not sure how, but I got her home without seeing her crash into a single parked car.

Next morning, we awakened to the joyful sound of a young woman doing the "pre-date ballet," and she fairly danced into our bedroom.

"Daddy! A man called!"

She bounced around our bedroom laughing and humming. We laughed with her. We were constantly teasing her about her boyfriends, because they usually seemed weird. And she did not have very many, so it was always easy to pick the weird ones. But she was consistently so far ahead of her peers that she seemed to pick weird just to be entertained.

Elizabeth had graduated from home school very early and started college locally at age 16. She was a junior at Utah State when she just got plain tired and came home. It was Christmas time, and she was lonely.

This is a talented girl. She had done more than most kids. She picked up a violin and in six weeks was playing in an orchestra. She signed in two languages (for the deaf). She loved physics. And in my view, she needed some play time.

Now she was home playing, and she planned to do it for a couple of months. This particular young fellow was a good man, but one I felt was from a badly dysfunctional family. Heck, I was from a badly dysfunctional family, so there are worse things (maybe I should ask my family, eh?). I had done the dad thing and discussed her options with this guy. She giggled over my concern and told me she did not intend to marry him.

"Yeah, well one of these days yer gonna look at me and say, 'Oops, Dad… did I mention we are married?' And then what will you say?"

"Dad you worry too much!"

Anyway, as she danced around, she told us the young man had asked her horseback riding. I asked if he had ever been riding, and she said no. We hooted over that, and I asked if he knew she was an expert horsewoman. She giggled and said no.

I told her I had given him a test, and he had recognized a horse three times out of five. I told her that on two occasions he had thought it was the biggest dog he had ever seen, and the ugliest.

She laughed and pounced on our bed and began to poke me in the ribs. I told her to stop or I would really tell her about him, and she shrieked!

I told her if he ever saw a horse's teeth, he might be scared. I told her he would probably try to feed his dog a biscuit but would not understand why she fed hers a carrot. My wife warned her if his horse were black and white, it better not say "moo." I reminded her if his horse were black and white, he might not understand the significance of "moo," but even he would be able to figure out it was not a dog. She first glared at me, then burst into laughter.

This is a happy, thoughtful Christmas for me. After all, it isn't all decorations, presents and work for the poor. Sometimes it is just loving.

Hey … 'tis the season to be jolly!

Chapter 5

On the Lessons of Life

A Lousy Millionaire

Every now and then I stop to ponder my options in the event I should suffer sudden, complete and irreversibly filthy wealth. Sadly, I have discovered that my high-tech tastes have pretty much fallen prey to my environment.

Should I be lusting after fancy cars? My high-performance milestone in cars was a Ford Falcon station wagon with a six-cylinder engine and three-on-the-tree. But, oh baby, could I put a shine on that old bomber!

Anyway, what would I do if I had a million dollars? As I have pondered it, I fear my simple life has really taken even my basic desires into captivity. The only thing I can relate to when I think of a million dollars is a great big pile of ten-dollar bills.

Think about it! Oh, I know we could all use a bunch of tens, but I lose sight of much over a thousand dollars. I just can't seem to think of much more than that and keep my perspective.

First thing, I'd probably go out and buy a new ... Ford, maybe ... probably a fancy one, such as a Fairlane or something like it, for my wife. (What do you mean? I am pretty sure they still make them. Don't they?) And a good used car for work.

And what constitutes a good used car to a millionaire? To this millionaire, it would require 25 miles per gallon or better, nice looking interior (not torn; I hate to sit on bare foam rubber or upholstery with holes in it), and a radio you can hear over the road noise. (Both speakers have to work, and the knobs must still be attached.) Maybe it would have an air conditioner, and if I were lucky, less than 100,000 miles on it. It shouldn't burn much oil and should get at least 10,000 miles on a set of tires. The windshield should have nothing worse than little cracks in it, and it would be just terrific if the speedometer and the overhead light worked.

And just what else would I get? I might go out and buy a new suit, 'cause there is a sale at Penny's this week. I would, for sure, have three sets of shoes I could wear in public, and I would probably replace my old running shoes just so everyone in the locker room will stop offering me foot powder.

I'd put another room on the house, and maybe another bathroom. I would add another coat of paint, maybe pay someone to do it. That dang vinyl exterior stuff is just too expensive for us mortals.

ON THE LESSONS OF LIFE

I'd probably give up my day-job to write full-time, but I would not buy a new word processor until I was able to eat on my writing ability. It looks as though it may be awhile before that happens, though.

I would buy that package education deal for each of my kids, right here in Alabama. I don't want them going north to school and turning into "carpet baggers," as my grandmother used to call those darn Republicans.

I would probably hire a maid so my sweet wife could get a break a couple of times a week. I'd buy her a flower every day. And I'd take her out every single Friday, probably to some place where they still bring food to the table. If she wanted seconds or dessert, I wouldn't have to worry about the budget. After all, she had six of my kids, and mean as she is, she sure deserves it.

My wife has a few quirks, and I'd pander to each one. She likes opals, so I would get her several. But I'd buy her a rock the size of Gibraltar and make her wear it just so I could say she has one. Even then, when I'd go somewhere with a rich friend (I'm sure if I were rich, I'd have a rich friend, wouldn't I?), I'd probably lie and say it was just some of her old jewelry and tell him that he should see the big one back in the safe.

I think I'd have to practice this part of acting rich a little while before I could get the hang of it.

I'd buy her a fur of some kind, but I am not sure Alabama has enough cold weather to justify wearing one. So if it happens, she'll just have to be hot.

I have some old bib overalls she hates because, she says, they're worn out. I'll probably have to break down and get new ones. And I suppose she'll make me get some new pajamas you can't read through, too.

I am afraid I may not have a very progressive outlook in the world of high finance, either. I don't trust folks who claim to have the answers in stock options, bonds, tax shelters and the like. But I would make do somehow. In fact, in an odd twist, I actually made a great deal of money because I could not afford to put money in the stock market. So when they lost so much money, I was better off than many of my peers. Anyway, today I'd put a lot of my money in the bank and in savings bonds, hire an old-fashioned accountant and maybe dabble in raising some farm animals.

I would probably still not buy my next dog, especially since the animal shelter still has all those "free" animals. But knowing I could afford it would allow me to be more selective before I would rush to take one home.

I would have steak once a week, no matter what those darn doctors say (all of them Democrats, you can be sure). And I would ensure it had enough sodium, cholesterol and saturated fats to taste good.

I would never let my wife make pizza again. I would call out for it and pay a serious tip, so next time I called the service would be terrific! And any time I wanted, I would go by the Dairy Queen and get one of those delicious chicken sandwiches that are always on special.

I would still expect my kids to work through college. But I would buy them a thousand-dollar car instead of a five-hundred-dollar car to drive, if they stayed in line.

I would buy a new couch, an easy chair and a second TV. I might even buy a second VCR.

I would make a list of every money grubber who came to my door for a handout and publish it in a local paper. I would feed any man who came to me hungry and jail any man who lied about it.

Yeah. You're right. I'd probably be a rotten millionaire.

But if I had to start over and could still choose a wife and kids and in-laws, and if I could somehow see my family, why, I'd give the whole million and all I could mortgage to have the ones I got.

A Child's Understanding

On our property, to our never-ending dismay, pine needles and pinecones are forever needing to be picked up from our yard. It is one of the few chores with which every child can help. The kids take great joy in gathering pinecones and needles into great piles so they can jump into them.

On one particular Sunday in church, my sweet wife was singing in the choir, so I was handling our six kids. I was doing pretty well, if I do say so myself. I was taking full credit for Nancy's quiet nature (a departure from forever squirming and turning during church) when I noticed her face wrinkled into a puzzled frown.

"Dad," she whispered, "what is wrong with that lady?" She pointed bashfully.

"Which one?" I asked as I twisted around to see a friend of ours in the pew behind us. She was wearing a bandage on her face, about one inch by two inches, just below her left eye.

"Oh. Looks like she has a boo-boo, doesn't it?"

Suddenly, a tiny light seemed to come on behind that poker-face. Nancy nodded solemnly.

"Musta fell on a pinecone or something," she declared firmly.

Mentoring a Boy Scout

Peer pressure makes it tougher than ever these days for a kid to balance his judgment in deciding what he should and should not do. The decision process leading to action seems to depend more on the "cool" than on the merit of an activity. That's partly why it is so tough to stamp out such activities as drug use and alcohol abuse. Peer pressure can be a deadly force in the life of a youth.

ON THE LESSONS OF LIFE

We adults forget how important it is to share some practical insight into the true merits of popularity. A young person has great difficulty thinking past his peer-influence to the consequences. And a good teaching moment may well be used by a respected adult to set an example or to gain trust, which can be used for later influence.

I had such a moment when a boy met me for a ride to a Boy Scout outing. I had just returned from two weeks in an Army field exercise. He was not ashamed to be seen with me this day because I had returned in a flight suit (almost the absolute top-of-the-line in "macho cool") and needed a shave (just the right touch).

He was very "in crowd," a kid who hated bib overalls, work days at home, old fashioned dads and especially adult supervision. I was the classic example of all these, and he felt bitter sympathy for my own sons. Being blessed with all wisdom, this kid would often banter with me over such things as the way I dressed and the way I did stuff with (or to) my sons. He was bold, but as polite as he knew how to be. And he certainly considered himself a match to my feeble wit.

On this day he spied two points of etiquette he felt needed comment.

First, I was wearing the old two-piece flight suit, and it diminished my image in his eyes.

These old two-piece suits were widely rejected as not as "cool" as the new one-piece suits. The one-piece flight suit had originally been Air Force-only issue. It was a macho sage-green color and had a sort of fighter-pilot image associated with it. For years the Army had refused to use the one piece and had issued the baggy, saggy looking, two-piece green flight suits, looking more like the fatigues of ground soldiers. Initially, the new suit was very popular among Army pilots, since it went without saying that every Army pilot knew such a suit made you fly better.

Having subscribed to this line of reasoning, the kid was absolutely unimpressed by my assertion that bodily functions in the cold and black of night are a lot less complicated (and a lot warmer) with a two-piece flight suit with trousers that come off without removing the shirt and jacket. I didn't burden him with the lesson I learned the first time I tried to use that one-piece flight suit in the aforementioned manner ... and pooped on my sleeve.

Second, he thought my plastic C-Ration spoon, carefully tucked into the pencil pocket on my sleeve, was tacky.

"Why, even Rangers carry them," I said, knowing how he envied Ranger esprit. "Besides, you never can tell when this ol' spoon might come in handy."

Now, this young man hated to be dirty, sticky, yucky, or in any way uncool.

Because he expected to ride about 45 minutes, I pulled out a cup of his favorite food in the world: ice cold cherry yogurt. This kid was known to howl at the moon for some of this stuff, and when I had opened it and had my spoon at the ready, I pretended to just notice his mournful look. I handed it over wordlessly, and put the spoon back.

"Say ... would you mind ... lending me the spoon?" he whined.

"Why?" I asked innocently.

"I'll get all sticky," he said.

"Tacky. I think you said tacky," I said, teasing him.

"No," he corrected immediately. "This is sticky." he pointed at his cup.

"And tha—" he pointed at the spoon, and, suddenly aware of his predicament, finished in a whisper ... "is tacky."

I continued to refuse the spoon, so he happily began to drink what yogurt he could and scrape out the rest with his fingers. Half-way there he was trying to lick off his fingers and prepared to wipe them on the universal Boy Scout napkin: his shirt.

I clucked my disapproval.

"Ants," I grunted.

He began to look around nervously.

"At the campsite," I said. "You don't want ants, do you?"

So he sat there for 20 minutes, open-fingered, trying not to touch anything until he arrived. Then he slinked off, unseen, and washed his gooey hands.

When I saw him that evening, he had slipped a spoon of his own into his shoulder pocket, and one of the boys asked him if he wasn't trying to be like the "old man."

"Him?" he sneered. "You've got to be kidding. Didn't you know that Rangers always carry a spoon? Never can tell when it might be handy!"

I winked at him. He smiled and walked away.

Now the lesson here is not complicated. We adults all know the popular way is not always the best way. And when you tell that to a kid, he may or may not believe you.

But if you can show him your world is really the one he sees, make him believe that it is the one he wants to be in, that it makes you happy, and that you put on no airs, he will learn to trust you. Once he does, you are in a position to mentor him. Just ask a good dad.

I can't tell you this principle works on all young men. But I know it makes some of the finest Boy Scouts in the world.

Choose Carefully Your Friends

Isn't it amazing how quickly a man takes offense if it is convenient to do so? It is so much easier to growl at a man who is an enemy rather than one who is a friend. When peers expect a man to take offense over one thing or another, he nearly always does. Then without thinking twice, he often takes the action his peers seem to indicate is appropriate. He is often disappointed by the consequences of his actions.

Choose your friends carefully. Act with forethought, and refuse to be offended. Your reward will be genuine happiness.

The Joy in a Little Boy's Heart

He was a skinny little runt of a kid when his family packed up and moved from a dairy farm in western New York to the wild and wooly town of Phoenix, Arizona.

He had always been little and timid, which made him wonderful to Mom, and a bit of a sissy to Dad. The family opened up a small restaurant in the new town. He played some and ate regular, but he just couldn't understand what the heck they could do there without cows. It was lucky they had a big silver thing that gave milk.

First summer there, he became covered in blisters. Head to foot, wherever there was bare skin, there were bare blisters. The doctor said he was allergic to the sun. So he had to stay indoors more than he wanted. A lot more.

Then Daddy went broke. The boy didn't know exactly what that meant, since when the lamp fell over, it was broken; but when little brother fell over, he was hurt, not broke. Whatever else it meant to go broke, it meant they would have to leave. They were sad, and it was awfully confusing. It was a hard time.

So they moved to a dirty little town where you could saddle up the cockroaches and ride them to a rattlesnake rodeo. A little place called Somerton, Arizona.

Somerton wasn't the end of the world, but you could see it from there. It was a little border town where the kids were rougher than any he had ever known.

MOBY DAD I: ADVENTURES IN LIVING

Dad seemed disappointed in his son because he was so timid. He wouldn't fight, didn't mix well with other kids. A lot of them spoke Spanish, you see, and they were hard to understand. The boy got through it. But it was still pretty bleak in the eyes of a little boy.

One day a bookmobile came through town, right out back of the house. It opened up a whole new world. First time he ever saw that lumpy, fat, bus-looking thing, he wasn't too excited. But he went in once and never missed it after that.

There was such a response to that bookmobile effort that a wonderful lady in town stepped up and volunteered to be the librarian to whatever library the town could muster. Muster they did, somehow, and the boy entered his first real world of books.

Her name was Grace Shipp, wife of the local banker, mom of the prettiest girl in town. The mom sang in the church choir and lived on a better side of town. But little people seemed to be her joy. The boy didn't know it, but she was his hero.

Mrs. Shipp began to guide him. She knew he loved animals, so she let him read about them. The animals in these books talked. They were pals; they had problems and worked them out. There were rabbits, beaver, deer and bear. They had fun and adventure. When the boy outgrew them, there were others. Then horses became his true love, and Walter Farley had wonderful adventure books of the Black Stallion and the Island Stallion, and … then there was Nancy Drew, of all people. And the Hardy Boys. There were stories of brave men, war stories, flying stories and happy and sad stories. Archery, shooting, model airplanes, history, fishing. You could learn to do anything from a book, if you got the right book.

The boy grew up and became a Marine, then an Army pilot. He grew up with horses, and animals have always been a part of his life. But books, and writing—they are the joy of his heart.

I was that little boy. I may not remember those days too clearly, or even the way they really were. But I will always remember my love for this gentle, caring lady who changed my life and the lives of so many others. She is retired now, but in my mind's eye, on a sleepy Wednesday afternoon, I can still stand on my toes, peer over and see her behind that huge desk. She is asking for the library card I never remembered, not even needing the number to sign out my books.

Thank you, Mrs. Shipp.

The Ability to Communicate

Of all the mortal powers, the ability to communicate is least understood. That talent can change John Doe into the purveyor of great ideals, make him known for generations and create from his words a legend.

The McDonald's hamburger chain has a better working knowledge of this principle than the entire balance of world powers.

Signs of the Times

Imagine, if you will, the strange things all around us that indicate our real situation in life. In my opinion, we as a society, have been sleeping peacefully through these real indicators for centuries, and only recently have found them to be valuable. Today, in modern police work, we have started to use many of them as we develop the technology.

For example, finger prints. How many real assassins could have been identified if the world at that time could have compiled a criminal file system and used fingerprints?

How about photographs? The valuable "first on the scene" photos of the murder of Caesar, of great battles, even of George Washington, could be used to reexamine old conclusions, to allow scholars to re-think history. Hannibal might have a wart on his nose, or Columbus might be really ugly, in a friendly sort of way.

Or how about hair? I saw a study based upon hair samples (sent out to his admirers by a very vain Napoleon), which indicate he was poisoned, and thus murdered.

The list goes on. For example, body heat. A special infra-red technique can identify the location and chronological place a warm-blooded body occupied in a house, even after his departure.

Let's apply this precept to my home. A world class investigator, on the order of Sherlock Holmes, enters my house to learn what he can of my family, who is, we'll say, gone. Missing. Not a clue as to their whereabouts.

What will he think of a stale bit of food in the refrigerator? Is it possible it was forgotten there? Did someone just pitch it in there to help Mom in the after-dinner clean-up? How about the wreckage in the bedrooms? Or in the kitchen? Has there been a kidnapping? A murder?

"First of all," I can imagine the sleuth saying, "all that speculation is wrong. Judging by the number of unmatched socks lying on the bedroom floors, I can see that at least six kids live here."

"Next," he would go on, "that food, if it was much good to begin with, must have been served with some other wonderful tidbit or it would never have made it to the refrigerator. Barring that, if it made it to the refrigerator at all, Mom probably put it there, so the kids wouldn't know about it until school was out next day. Then even stale food would vanish.

"This bit of stale food was not really food anyway. It was being saved for mouse bait or some such venture. Proof of that is that there is not a can of pop, a cookie, a bowl of ice cream … not one crumb is to be found outside of lock and key.

"And see all those dirty dishes? One meal and a day's after-school treats, or maybe supper and breakfast. They left here well fed.

"What's that, Watson? The wreckage in the bedrooms? Well, in four of those bedrooms, the hormones are raging. I can tell by the deodorant, lipstick, after-shave and shaving gear, soccer and football stuff, idols on the walls, baseball cards, dollies and little toy cars scattered around.

"Seems as though these kids might have gone to school today, except for the books, papers and reports lying around. We are getting close now, Watson. Look here. There are only 10 towels per kid left in this closet. That plus the absence of swim suits and sun screen, and all the flip-flops are all missing … Why, look … there's no Kool-Aid, and all the ice trays are empty. And Dad's extra large (one-fat-size-fits-all) swimsuit is missing!

"That's it, Watson! They're at the beach! They left early. No one saw them. They either took a lot of food or a lot of money to feed those dang kids. Dad must have promised to wash the dishes tonight if Mom would just leave it all."

There you have it. Nothing is sacred. You just can't keep a secret anymore.

A Father's Prayer

Lord, this morning I dropped my son off at a friend's home to go to the Scout Encampment. I sort of choked this one off, since it occurred to me for the first time that he was growing up.

Anyway, he went off to camp without so much as a look back. As well as I know the place of adventure in a boy's life, I shall worry over him until he learns to manage his risk. I know kids will get hurt, even die under the most peculiar circumstances. But most of the time, if they will simply not take a headlong rush to get somewhere, they will not suffer serious injury.

Lord, protect my sons and daughters. I think they will contribute to your program on this earth. But I fear they will be nearly as foolish as their father before they learn the genuine values of this life.

You have protected me from certain death and serious injury several times. If I have done any of Thy work, protect my descendants.

Prove them by fire, but allow them a place in your Kingdom. Do not let my faults weigh them in their eternal progress, and do not let my attitude toward work damage their fragile personalities. Help me to remember they are only children, and to be patient with their efforts.

If You need one of them, I will have nothing to complain about. They have been mine to love and hold for such a wonderfully long time. But I would prefer if You need one of us, that you take me. I may not be as good, but I will work like a mule, and I will gratefully accept whatever chore needs to be accomplished, if it may be that You will preserve them on this earth a little longer.

And I have one last favor, if You wouldn't mind my asking. I would give all I am and all I may ever be, and all I will ever have, to have my wife there, in that kingdom we hear so much about. She gave me my family, she kept me on the straight track. Forever without her would be just another form of hell to me.

Besides, if I were without her, you wouldn't be getting much of a bargain.

The Joys of Owning a Jalopy

Rejoice! All backyard mechanics and patriarchs of numerous progeny, gather near! The joys of owning an old car are many, and at times like this (my baby is in the shop), these joys need some airing. See if this doesn't ring true!

I paid $700 for my car 100,000 miles ago. It is ugly; the horn works only when the sun has shone on the dash awhile; and both radio knobs are missing. Only one speaker works, and the antenna is broken. Seats are mostly foam rubber and the seat covers expired long ago, with only the backs retaining much fabric. The windshield is cracked, and the air conditioner doesn't work anymore.

If I'm lyin', I'm dyin'. Honest. One of my friends is so embarrassed over her that he has offered repeatedly to paint her. But I love that car.

We both know there are a lot of advantages of owning an old car, don't we? First of all, if it is old enough and cheap enough, there are no payments. But it gets better. Mere money could never explain our love for the old jalopy.

I have found that upkeep on an old, reliable car is a lot less than car payments, and after the first year, even a new car (with payments) requires upkeep. New car parts and new car technology costs more than old car parts, generally.

Insurance for an old ugly car is easy. I mean, if you go in and tell the insurance agent you have a bright red, late-model Corvette, he is only too happy to take your money (as much as he can carry). But go in, describe the car you wish to insure as "… a dumpy, old, rusty gray car and I'm sorry, I can't remember what kind it is." Then the agent, who makes his money on commission, looks out the window at your junker, goes outside to look it over and comes back in mourning. That's when you know the rates won't get any better.

Return on your investment in a clunker is excellent. Once as I tried to sell one of my old crates, no one seemed to want it. After several weeks of local advertising, I jacked the price up to $500—I told you this was a crate—and put a sign on it: "Old. Ugly. Burns oil. $500."

No kidding. It sold in 12 hours.

There is also a certain confidence that the old car will not only be where you left it, but it will be in generally the same condition.

One day I noticed a car parked next to mine. The owner walked up to her car and glared at my bomber. Then she carefully inspected her car for paint damage she suspected I might have inflicted on her shiny new(er) car with my door.

"Careful!" I cautioned her. She straightened up, surprised to see me there.

"Be careful!" I told her again. Startled, she looked around to be sure I was speaking to her.

"What?"

"Watch your door. Don't scratch my paint," I growled obnoxiously.

She was dumbstruck, and as I walked away, she fiddled nervously with her keys. She got in carefully and left quickly.

And last but most important, I expect that my cheap cars are going to help me pay the freight of college for six mean, hungry kids.

Now, getting a great deal on an old car has its disadvantages. For example, once my wife bought a sweet old Suburban, cheap. I mean, it looked great, had chrome running boards, good paint and a very clean interior.

We drove home that year, pulled into Grandpa's driveway and noticed that he had planted short telephone poles around the inner radius, with chain strung attractively around the yard. Anyway, second day there, my wife clipped a post with the running board. Needless to say, that shiny, new running board didn't have a prayer. It folded like tin foil and didn't even chip the post. Instead of moaning as I would have expected, she came bouncing into the house and cheerfully told me the good news, "… and … well … that's why we spent $3500 and not $35,000 on that sucker!"

I was really steamed, and my bright red ears were a clear precursor to a big blow.

Dad, knowing he had groomed me to appreciate a good used car, wasted no time in springing the trap. His sympathy was not quite what I was hoping for.

"Well, son, seeing how you have saved over $30,000 or so today, how about taking us to dinner?"

Youth

I wrote this after an aircraft accident in my unit.

Youth is a wonderful thing. It is simply not enough. The tragedy affects us all when a young aviator goes down. It could have been any one of us. I believe this risk, and the lack of it in nearly all other endeavors, is the source of the common bond of aviators. Life is short, and it is sweet.

Whatever your mark will be in the world, now is the time to make it.

On Picking Your In-laws

I was a wild-eyed-pirate sort of kid when my parents picked up all we owned and moved to the western New York town of Holland.

It was my senior year, and I was enraged and embittered. After all, I had been an ugly duckling sort all through high school. I had worked my butt off trying to gain some popular status, and now this. In one sweep, I had lost my job, my girl and my popularity.

MOBY DAD I: ADVENTURES IN LIVING

I came to Holland, chip on my shoulder, to show them Easterners what was what, and … well, anyway, I met a kid who would become a very good friend, Jay Fancher.

Jay was also a wild sort of kid, and we quickly became good friends. He was a year younger, but I was too obnoxious for the more popular fellow classmates of Holland Central. So there was none of the usual "separate class" mentality between us.

I became a part of his family, and his dad was a heck of a man. Quietly, Dad Fancher began to entice the better part of me to the more serious side of life. Mom Fancher, knowing I needed some taming and guidance, spent many nights up late in her kitchen, just talking with me about the mysteries of life. She liked me and would jerk my chain in the moment when I needed to pay attention. Good thing.

Dad taught me to play chess; Jay, Dad and I would often spend Friday or Saturday night into the wee morning hours playing. I think I beat Dad three times in my life. That counts all the times I won when he spotted his queen, which were too numerous to mention.

Their family was tolerant of my occasional excesses, like the time I got a bit tipsy and sang and spoke all the parts to the musical "Kiss Me Kate" on their kitchen floor.

Some of it was standing.

Some of it was sitting.

Some of it was spent crawling around the floor, trying to get on to the next part.

I went off to college and then joined the Marine Corps. One day, on leave and preparing for what I expected was only a stop enroute to Vietnam, I discovered that the Fanchers had daughters.

The one I met was cute, and she was Jay's sister, so she couldn't be too bad. Anyway, she was pretty young, so I was careful to approach Dad before I dated her. He gave his solemn approval, and I grew to be really nuts about her. Too bad. She dumped me.

I came home on leave and a miracle happened. She loved me again. So, okay, off I go to another stop I considered only a temporary assignment enroute to Vietnam (I never did get there). All was well until her younger sister (I swear I hardly knew she was alive) wrote and told me she was to be the maid of honor at my girl's wedding.

Funny, I remember thinking. I hadn't thought about planning so far ahead. In fact, I hadn't been thinking too clearly at all when it became clear from the letter that the wedding would occur in my absence. Suddenly I realized that her wedding was unlikely to involve me at all. Darn it all, anyway.

I was really peeved, this time. No more Mister Nice Guy. If yer gonna marry someone else, then we're through. And that's that! How do ya like them apples anyway, eh, honey? That'll show her. I'll bet she never marries anyone else again. Put that in your pipe and smoke it!

I went home on leave with another one of those chips on my shoulder, you know, to settle up with the jerk she married. (Honest, I had no clue that I was probably the biggest jerk in those parts.) I was still pretty miffed about the whole situation.

I arrived home and was rummaging around Jay's place one afternoon when Mom jerked my chain again. She had a remarkable insight into my potential, certainly a better understanding of it than I had. She ran me off to get Baby Sister a soda. One thing led to another. I was real nervous about this one.

Dad gave me the evil eye again, grunted his approval, and a year later, I got the best in-laws in the world.

Young men everywhere, prepare yourselves. Plan, scheme, connive and lie, but get a great set of in-laws. Do whatever it takes. As I did.

Well … there may be some key points you will want to refine in the use of this technique.

Dreams

There are very few impossible dreams. Most of them are merely unpursued reality.

The Price

Personal sacrifice seems often to be such a high price that men refuse to pay it. But it is always the down payment required for each of man's sweetest, most rewarding experiences.

Preparation

The position a man occupies is the momentum with which he affects the world. Quite often his mere presence (or absence) in a location or position will afford him opportunity to achieve a goal, a success or a genuine greatness. Perhaps even one to which he may not aspire.

Even gods cannot wrestle for a prize without an opportunity to lay hold of the opponent.

Prepare for the moment! Opportunity may show her face only once.

Couch Potato for President

Couch Potatoes, unite! Pick up your remotes, your extra-large and baggy sweat suits, your pretzels and potato chips, get on your riding lawn mowers, pack up your good books and join me in a march to the White House. I will be a president who can represent all of us! We shall prevail!

Are you tired of being laughed at because you are of a naturally easy nature? Have you been mistaken for lazy because you like the intellectual things, such as good food, good books and good music, rather than the "macho" pastimes such as sports or chewing tobacco?

Do you want a president who cannot be flawed for his moral character or foreign policy?

I am that man. The worst any woman can say about me is that I am really homely, and the worst that can be said of my foreign policy is that I want a tariff on every Japanese car.

How about special interests? I can honestly say I have special interest in lots of stuff: When did my kid take his last shower? How are his grades? Has Lewis Grizzard really had three wives? Do Moon Pies go on sale this week? Who really picks some of the idiots on Oprah? Or on Merv Griffin, for that matter? And how do you think they find those jerks, day after day, anyway?

Join me in declaring our rightful place in the leadership of this great nation! Together we shall remove those disgusting TV ads about weight loss programs. We will organize research on the relative merits of good eating and provide counter-propaganda to all those health pamphlets we see around doctors' offices.

We shall pass a Couch Potato Equal Rights bill and insist on one couch potato anchor man for each television station. You can see some of the success of our lobby in the appointment of Jingles, cowboy sidekick to the old TV hero Wild Bill Hickok!

Come with me! I will now refuse to feel shamed by a waist size significantly larger than my inseam. Our platform will take pride in the way we eat to maintain our physical stature and cheery disposition.

ON THE LESSONS OF LIFE

The Pillsbury Dough Boy will be our mascot for the time being. I can foresee that a serious burst of the popularity in a party that might lead us to claim something more recognizable, like a talking horse or a happy looking dog. But I promise we will never lay claim to the donkey or the elephant!

No more of the beached whale jokes while we're lying out for a tan. The in-crowd will say, in awe, "Now there lies a couch potato."

No more will we fall prey to the medical profession (most of them Republicans, anyway) who insist that we eat "healthy foods low in cholesterol, saturated fats and sodium," and which, by default, are generally tasteless.

No more will we be made to feel guilty by the careless words of health nuts (most of them Democrats), who insist on exercise and fitness inflicted by hours of running, jumping, walking, bicycle riding, skating, skiing and other sports that leave you feeling something like "The Agony of Defeat."

No more! My sweat pants are going to start wearing out the way they ought to—seat first! My running shoes will be antiques before I purchase another pair! In our party the word "sweat" will become a word used to describe only lather on a horse or the lack of effort in one of our many vast accomplishments!

As the founding member of CPAA (Couch Potatoes Anonymous of Alabama), I have decided to come out of the closet, run for president and claim the rightful place for couch potatoes in all walks of life.

I hereby lay claim, by default, to the chairmanship of the Couch Potato Party. I am certain, given the current records (and stature) of our Honorable Senators and Representatives, and the popularity of our laid-back platform, that I can easily convert many of them to our cause. Heck, it won't take much more effort than they are putting out right now.

Even more certainly, a party platform that takes the sugar off the promises (no bun intended) and delivers little more than nothing should do well, if honest voters consider the comparative performance of the donkey and the elephant this election year! Spread the word!

In Search of Qualified Leadership

The really difficult jobs occur when some lofty knothead dreams up solutions to problems he simply does not understand. That does not always have to happen.

Suppose in the Beginning, the Lead Angel had decided cows' legs were insufficient transport and, without thinking or checking with the Boss, cows were made to fly.

Think about it. What implications would that have for the FAA? OSHA? Why, dairy farmers, ranchers, other birds and innocent bystanders below would have serious alternatives to consider.

And every toast, as they raise the cup to the sky, would have to include, "… and here's mud … or whatever … in your eye."

Leaving Your Mark

In order for a man to leave his mark on the world, he must displace some of the current momentum with his own initiative. It may not be easy or popular. It requires sacrifice and hard work. None of that effort matters.

The alternative is to be swept along the stream of life like a fish.

You Can Be My Kid Any Time

In my spare time I do some volunteer work as a secretary for a fairly large church organization. There is always someone to do for, as there was one day recently.

I arrived late, and I found a little girl quietly minding her own business, sitting on the little couch in our waiting room, drawing. Her mom was not around, so I assumed correctly that she was there to discuss something with one of our leaders that afternoon.

As I walked in, she took immediate notice and sat up straight. I could almost hear the wheels turn. I was a man, she was a little girl. She was not sure what I was up to. But I acted like I was supposed to be there, and she went back to drawing.

Mom took a long time. I regularly have to watch little ones who must be unattended for a few moments, so I am accustomed to it. I handle all the little emergencies like "...

where's the bathroom", or "...can I come in there and see yer office, Mister?". But she didn't move, and seemed a little distant as she drew.

I felt she was kind of lonely, so I went out and sat in a chair near her. I didn't even get a nod, so I started admiring her work. I asked her name, and she told me.

We'll call her Constance (not her real name), but she soon corrected me. Connie would do, she said, and she was tickled to think I would ask. I asked if she always drew that well, and she beamed. She was only six, she said proudly, and she was REAL bored. But she drew a lot.

"First grade is tough," she said. "Last year I only thought kindergarten was hard," she went on. "This year it was really tough."

Are you married, I asked. She giggled. "Six. I'm only SIX, remember?" Oh, yeah. It was hard to tell.

Do you like your teacher, I asked. Oh yes, she said. She said she hardly ever gets her name on the board, but she has to really watch it. She likes to talk.

Do you have any brothers or sisters? Not a one, she answered. "I have been talking to Mom about that..."

"Well, you sure are pretty. I'll bet you're the apple of your Daddy's eye, huh?"

She said nothing, but started drawing again.

ON THE LESSONS OF LIFE

Here, I have a picture of my wife, with my kids. Wanna see it, I asked? Sure, she said.

"See there? She's the mean one," I hooted.

She laughed. She asked how many kids as she counted them. Six, I answered, and we have a three-legged dog.

The dog was good for a few minutes more conversation. Then I went back to my office to work. She came in a few minutes later.

"Mama still isn't out," she said. "We haven't eaten yet. Do you think we will eat out?"

Probably, I answered. Maybe Dad will take you all out.

She was finally on the ropes, and I felt she wanted to tell me something. She did. She looked twenty-five.

"I don't think so. Mama is here... to talk about Daddy. He's... mean to us. I mean... other men, they love me. But he doesn't. And he hurts Mama."

I was unprepared for the feelings which flooded my heart in an instant. I was filled with rage that a six-year-old girl should have to stare down at such critical questions. I wanted to hold this little girl, protect her.

I choked it all down. I said nothing. I handed her a piece of paper, a pencil, and chatted with her until Mom was done with her business.

When Mom came out, I told her how sweet her daughter was, and showed her the picture she had drawn for me. She

had written a separate note on a yellow sticky, and pasted it to the picture. It said "I love You and God."

As they turned to go, I couldn't help it. I called one last time.

"Connie, you can be a kid at my house. Any time."

I wasn't kidding. And she knew it.

The Real Indicators

The real fiber of every man is clearly reflected in the fruit of his labor. Do not confuse this to mean that material success is the only or even the most effective indicator. His friends, family, hobbies, pursuit of education and initiative all point to his real character.

Working knowledge of this principle can provide a man with remarkable insight to his fellow man.

Summary of the Moment

When it is all said and done, when all the preparation is complete and the final moment has arrived, there is a famous quote that sums up the frivolous nature of the nobility in all human endeavors:

"Holy cow, Batman!"

Good Men Don't Glitter

I have seen bib overalls come and go in popularity, but they are pretty drab for the thrill seeker. And I think in today's society, bib overalls bring to mind someone who works with animals or someone who has a dirty job. Perhaps someone simple-minded—maybe someone like me.

MOBY DAD I: ADVENTURES IN LIVING

Only the sleek is acceptable in some circles of modern society, especially among the youth. As a pilot, I had someone tell me once that bib overalls didn't fit my image. I had a hard time with that. I think this country was built in bib overalls. To me, they symbolize a high work ethic in their no-frills practicality.

I was riding down the road recently when I noticed an old man working in a yard. He was at least 80, in old bib overalls, and he was going like blazes, rake in hand, raking leaves into a fire. Several kids were standing around, doing nothing, and a woman was watching him quietly. I took this in, and in a flash was concerned that he might work too hard.

While I watched, the woman came over and tried to help. He brushed her away. It was clearly his yard, his job, maybe his rake. I realized in an instant that it was his joy to do the work.

I know another great couple—not Mr. and Mrs. America—well, at least not the Mr. and Mrs. America the media sell to our kids. You know the ones I am talking about, with the perfect house, the perfect figure, the ideal job, the perfect marriage with two and 1/3 kids.

This couple I know are quiet folk with five kids. All of them are good kids. They have three old cars. He is a mechanic who dabbles in auctions on the side, and he even sells used cars. He is quiet. He loves his wife and kids.

I tease his wife about being a mean woman, but she is adored by her children. There are no airs there. No pretense. They live in an old trailer, paid for, neat and clean. Dad wouldn't know how to tell a lie, but he would be rude if you offended his family.

One day during a visit, I began to confide in this man, my friend. I talked about some of my secret dreams and problems. We talked about such things as money, sacrifice and kids. He began to share some of his own secrets.

He went to his secret place and pulled out a little metal box full of U.S. Savings Bonds—a whole lot of them. Heck, there was $24,000 in bonds that I saw, and more I couldn't see.

I was tricked for a moment into thinking he was only going to boast a bit. I began to choke off some worldly advice about how he could do better than putting all his money into bonds when he quietly began reciting a litany of reasons, almost apology, for the pile of bonds being so small.

He had bought a place down the road he said quietly. He got a great deal for cash, and with it paid for one kid's education. As he went on, this great, humble man whom I love so much, I heard nothing about anything that was for him or Mom. I really don't think he would feel comfortable in a new jacket or suit. No talk of a new car, no boat, no hobby or anything else to distract him. School for his kids, maybe even retirement someday, because he didn't want to burden anyone.

In fact, his greatest joy had nothing to do with selfishness; it was simply to work for these worthy goals. Here the work ethic of America is alive and well. And, I might add, it is in no danger of being stolen, at least in this little home. This man's life points to a long list of virtues we seem to forget.

The work ethic we all still admire on the surface is not really the philosophy most of us subscribe to anymore. We pretend it is so, but it isn't. Society has declared that the kids are too much bother, that we cannot afford them, that the community can find its own way without them, and has thought of work more like modern slavery than as a worthy part of life and living. We all gotta have a new car, a new house, a new gadget.

In the long term, our society will not get a lot better until we wake up and remember the whole spectrum of higher-level moral values is really a good thing. It is not simply a vain or foolish effort.

Integrity is essential to good living; virtue is not wimpy; our work is our investment in the future. Honesty is not naive foolishness; credit demands responsibility, and every action has a genuine consequence. Chastity is a virtue. Fidelity is an honorable prerequisite for a happy marriage. The choice may be made before the decision, but the consequences for most actions are unavoidable and cannot be blamed on society or some other person. The list goes on.

But on this day I have two boys who need to learn that good men don't glitter. I can only try to live up to the great example shown by my friend and hope it rubs off.

The Nature of God

I cannot pretend I know all about God. But I am convinced that without the office of fatherhood and motherhood, there would be no way for most mortals to fathom the concept of godhood, or the dictates every faith presents as those of God. The principles God employs seem far removed from the natural path of the carnal mind. It seems to me that parenthood naturally focuses noble purposes that seem similar to those of God. Perhaps it helps us mortals begin to understand God.

For example, pure love, which goes beyond rational bounds, is one of the first principles taught in the scriptures. Pure love in this context cannot be brought to any mind as quickly as to a parent's mind.

Forgiveness, a principle closely tied to compassion and unconditional love, is not possible for anyone as quickly as for a parent. Other principles, such as long-suffering, patience and love of innocent virtue are all veins of pure gold in the art of parenting, and they are very difficult to find in any other discipline.

The "joy in your posterity" promised by hopeful prophets does not imply that you will always be happy with your children. But there are great moments. Your child might make a gallant choice, and it will blind you with an odd rush of joy. Only parents know this feeling. It makes all your sacrifice a mere token payment on the real joy of it. You'll feel paid in full when someone says, "That daughter of yours was a perfect angel when I needed help."

The joy associated with these moments are known to all parents, but not comprehended by many. As I understand the scriptures, the greatest joy ever documented about God was that joy He felt for His Child. And His greatest anguish was over His Child. That sounds like a dad or two whom I have known. I know I'm repeating myself, but I think it's important enough to say again. I believe this joy and this anguish, those of parenthood, to be two of the "godly" attributes we are required to obtain in this life.

Society has lost touch with this concept. When asked what joys in life have made them truly happy, the answer for some parents oft times will not even include the place of children. Today, nearly half the couples in the United States who can have children choose not to. I think the world has lost its perspective of children and of the joys they bring. As a result, the world is a colder place.

It is strange how far removed from the Hollywood bedroom these joys are found, and how precious they are, how hidden from the world at large, how unassociated with common perceptions of real happiness, and how unappreciated in our modern culture. Rich men and poor men have basically the same chance to obtain children, and each makes his choices and his adjustments accordingly.

Few parts of modern society recognize the importance of these godly principles. As a result, I believe there is little real understanding of their importance in our lives. Maybe this misunderstanding of godly principles will explain the mystery most religions convey about the real nature of God.

The Real Measure of a Man

The episode of my experiencing an engine failure in my helicopter appears in a previous chapter. It was at night in a mountainous area, and I managed to save the aircraft. That account was written after I learned I would receive an award for my good fortune.

The difference between the image of king or pauper, hero or incompetent fool is often cast during the success or failure of one deed, usually over a small space in time, without any forethought or planning. Brave men and cowards are judged most often from a single act.

This image is often the purest, most distilled hokey-pokey. I honor brave, honest, faithful men of all kinds. But one act, one moment of action is a foolish measure of his character.

I believe the most accurate measure of a man is the adoration of his wife and the esteem of his children.

No fraud.

No pretense.

No peer pressure.

Only genuine love. Under such scrutiny, the real merit of a man can be seen without any problem.

Bonking!

Cross-country skiing is a tough sport. During the race, the skier works like mad to move down the trail until he is exhausted. This, the point of exhaustion, is known by cross-country skiers as "hitting the wall." Strategy for the race is to coast awhile, moving as well as possible without undue effort, until the skier's strength returns. Then the skier goes hard at it until he "hits the wall" again, and so forth, for the whole race. The term used to describe this phenomenon of repeated extreme exertion (or hitting the wall) is "bonking."

Tough as cross-country skiing is, it cannot compare to the stress of parenthood. Stay with me now.

Friday night came to my house, and I hoped after a week of school and activities, I was going to get a break. I planned to sweep my sweet wife away to dinner.

I got home to find Elizabeth (age 10), wanting to go to a friend's house for the night, and she asked, couldn't the friend please come for supper Sunday.

But Mom wasn't home yet from taking Jeff (age 16) to play practice, so I couldn't make a real decision until Mom gave the okay. (As you'll recall, I'm the boss in my house. Or at least I have permission to say so. But letting Mama know a few days before requiring her to feed company really helps keep my side of the bed warm at night.) It was a good thing I hesitated, because as it turned out, Mom declined.

ON THE LESSONS OF LIFE

Donny (age 14) had come home and been assigned two chores: clean up his room and mow the back yard. He was poking along at this effort when he got a call asking him to babysit at a friend's house. Sure, he said, and added that he would be ready as soon as they could pick him up. He was especially happy to eat their pizza rather than our broccoli-and-cheese casserole.

Nikki (age 13), our baby-sitter by default (because the oldest two now were busy) for this much-anticipated evening, now announced she had a different babysitting job, and since she had her job first, and since Mom knew all about it, she would go, and Donny would be in for the broccoli filled evening of fun and entertainment.

War was immediately declared, no prisoners to be taken, and both of them hissed and spat around the dining room table until I could get free to settle it.

Nancy (age seven) then fell off the trampoline and arrived at our back door with bloody nose in hand at the same moment Jeff called to say he had forgotten his costume. Mom had left him at the theater already; tonight's dress rehearsal would not happen and the world as we knew it would end if he did not have his whole costume.

Next, as if by coordination with the Dark Side, a friend called to ask if I were interested in taking my wife out with him and his wife for Chinese food, since it was Friday, and they were bored.

My wife then called from the Dairy Queen, where she had stopped for—get this—a flat tire, and asked couldn't I come and fix it so we could hurry and get away tonight.

"Okay, just as soon as I run the clothes to Jeff at the play practice, and oh, by the way, settle this fight with Donny and Nikki, will you?"

I summoned Nikki to the phone to let Mom exercise her sternest voice. I then raced out to the car and roared out of the driveway just as Mikie, my five-year-old, came running out in tears. I stopped, rolled down the window, and he cried:

"Kisses and hugs, Dad!"

A quick dismount for the kisses and hugs, then over to the theater, where Jeff had gotten embroiled in another practice session at a different location, which meant I had to hunt him down to give him his clothes.

Then off to the Dairy Queen where I managed to change the tire in record time but stained my shirt with tire-black. This provided cause for my sweet wife to critique my carelessness and lack of appreciation for her hard work cleaning and washing.

We got home, bolted to a local restaurant and ate very well. We then raced home and found the kids still up at 10 P.M., house destroyed, dinner table still dirty.

And as I collapsed into bed, world swimming before my eyes, I swear I could hear it in the distance.

Bonk!

ON THE LESSONS OF LIFE

Never Say Never: The Boat That Wouldn't Sink

For those of you who don't know the story, there was once a boat that was regarded as impossible to sink. It had all the latest features of safety, including the legally required number of lifeboats. The hull was specially designed with a double bottom and water-tight compartments throughout. It was boasted that three of these compartments could fail, and the ship would still float. It was the pride of the seas, and service onboard was wonderful. More crew cared for passengers than ran the ship, and the captain was over qualified almost to a fault, as was the entire complement of ship leadership.

The ship was, in fact, the third of a trio of ships built to capture the luxury corner of the passenger market between Europe and the United States. As such, it was the beneficiary of many improvements found in the flaws of the previous two. Passenger room was increased, size was increased, and special areas were made more roomy. The capacity for passengers was noted as exceeding the space of the lifeboats, but the law was obeyed and the truth ignored. The ship was unsinkable, after all, and the pride of the White Star lines. Thus began the legacy of the Titanic.

The Titanic was a bit less than a thousand feet long and about a hundred feet wide. It was fast, but not nearly the fastest ship afloat. The boat was popular and famous because of the lavish accommodations, but the real reason for White Star's interest in this liner was the huge passenger capacity. The second and third-class berths were roomy and pleasant and could carry a ton of people. The more people, the more money. The popularity of these liners meant they would capture a huge part of the second and third-class business, thus making more money. Fortunately, on its maiden voyage, it carried about 2,300 folks, far less than capacity.

Like all accidents, there were many "domino events" that had to fall into place before that boat sank. Prevention of any of them might have saved some or all of the people on that vessel.

For example, there could have been more life boats. That could have saved all 2,300 people. But the antiquated British law (it was American owned) required only so many boats per ton of displacement, and that law was fulfilled.

More of the lifeboats could have been full. That could have saved 500 more people. But as the investigations (several) established, not everyone was aware of the sinking until the boats were gone. Even many people who knew could not get to the boat area. In fact, some (mostly third class, from what I gather) were told to remain in quarters or were run off from the higher-class areas, where the boats were being launched.

Some of the half-full boats would not return to the wailing, freezing, drowning people still alive in the wake of the floundered ship. Those on the life boats were genuinely afraid of being swamped by panicked passengers in the water. At least one boat was overturned but stayed afloat. It returned and pulled all the survivors it could handle onboard before pushing off.

ON THE LESSONS OF LIFE

The captain could have ensured that his lookouts had binoculars. There are two stories about them. One says they were left behind on this voyage. The other says that one of the ship's officers was offended at being demoted to make room for another company officer, and in his haste to depart the ship, left the binoculars secured without anyone else knowing their location.

The captain was supposedly warned of a huge field of icebergs in his path, and he could have slowed his ship or detoured or, at least, not have been going 23 knots (more than 26 miles) per hour. It is not clear now that he was ever advised of the iceberg warnings. Then again, the ship could have hit the iceberg straight ahead, and amazingly, survived. Instead, it turned and slid along the 'berg, ripping a 300-foot gash along the starboard side. If the captain had opened the watertight compartments and leveled the ship, it would have floated an estimated six more hours. (It sank in less than two hours.) As it was, when the bow went under, the square-footage open to the sea increased exponentially, and it sank rapidly.

But there was another story, seldom told, and which in Titanic lore has no clear answers. It is the story of Captain Stanley Lord, of the ship Californian, which (depending on the witness), stood off in that field of ice between five and certainly less than 10 miles distant.

On the night of the disaster, the world seemed paralyzed by disbelief, complicated by misinformation. Disbelief because of the ship's reputation and misinformation because the wireless systems used by the Titanic and participating search ships were used poorly.

Morse code equipment was new, basically a novel hobby on the cutting edge of technology. As a novelty, Morse equipment was not considered critical to ships' sea-going function. They were weak, only a toy of the rich. Thus, it was that many amateurs claimed to communicate with the emergency vessels, and the media chains bought and published stories that were false, wrong, misconstrued or created for convenience.

Amid all the speculation of why and how and to whom, some of the crew's complement claimed to have seen another vessel in the vicinity and had, in fact, fired distress rockets and signaled distress by wireless and by Morse lamp. There was no response. But the search was on for the dirty dog who would ignore the call for help on the high seas.

Enter Captain Stanley Lord. A veteran with a sterling record, Captain Lord was the master of the 6,000-ton steamer Californian when he directed her to stop due to an unusual (huge) ice field. This was the ship accused of standing off in that field of ice between five and ten miles distant while the Titanic went down.

The official findings of the British and American inquiries, separate and unrelated to each other, were nearly identical in Captain Lord's condemnation. The discrepancies of logged times of sighting of the vessels by each other, some of the relative directions of the vessels sighted, his relative location as he had logged it, and his perception of the rockets as "company signals" (that is, not distress signals) were dismissed or ignored.

The case was thus: A vessel recognized as a large passenger vessel was seen by the Californian steaming into the ice field at a high rate of speed. Eight distress rockets were fired; the Californian saw eight. The times of different events were close. The ship sending rockets went out of sight about the same time the Titanic sank. The night was clear and the sea calm, and the Californian could have pushed through the ice to the rescue, but through a series of miscommunications and misunderstandings, the captain did not. Awakened from deep sleep several times, he did not recall some of the conversations with his crew. He never wakened the wireless operator, so he never heard the SOS (and CQD) distress signals. Making his position worse, he was a lousy witness, contradicting himself many times.

Captain Lord still has family and professional organizations trying to clear his name. Central to his case were several important points.

First, the position of both ships is highly questionable. During the hearings in 1912, this was not known, but the actual Titanic was found 10 miles from its officially recognized plot.

Second, the ship seen approaching the Titanic could not have been the Californian because at that time it is absolutely certain the Californian was "hove to" in the ice field.

Third, survivors on the Titanic lifeboats could not find the sighted ship, and the Californian was certainly stopped all that time.

Fourth, the times, and even the sequence of events really do not match, no matter how hard you try. Not the sightings, not the rockets, nothing.

Fifth, none of the rockets exploding were heard on the Californian, which indicates a distance greater than the suspected five to 10 miles.

Last, the captain had everything to win and nothing to lose by going to the rescue, as he proved by going directly to the search area as soon as he realized the situation.

Reasonable doubt was never even considered. Captain Lord lost his job. His career was in the dumper.

Today we know exactly where the Titanic rests. The wreck has been examined. I have read a dozen books on this sensational subject. I even purchased a paperback copy of the American Congressional investigation. For all the money made by the authors speculating on the how and why of the events leading to the demise of the Titanic, the most accurate record seems to be the 1912 United States Senate Investigation. Their conclusions stunk, but the facts were pretty much captured for future evaluation.

In the end, another company took Lord on and got a bargain. Captain Lord had 15 years more sterling service as a ship's captain before retiring.

He died declaring his innocence.

On Chasing Illusions

I have a great friend, Al, whom I have known for several years. This guy is a peculiar sort. For starters, he is a genius—a bored genius it seems, but still well attached to the sane and practical world. At 66 he's smart as a whip and strong as an ox. He is amazing.

To start with, he retired to "a little place" in the country (a 5,000-foot ranch-style house on 80 acres), bought a few books and set up a farm operation.

Well, one thing led to another. He bought one old truck, then another. Next, he leased and purchased a couple of hundred more acres. He bought an old tractor, then another. Today he runs 50 or so cows, including doing all the physical things that go with keeping cattle. Now he's bought a rental property and keeps that up. Well, you get the picture. He does this in his spare time. Ha! Before he retired, he was a full-time engineer, doing all this on the side.

Al is never still. His greatest joy is to ask some young stud to help him just to see if he can wear the kid down. Pat him on the back and he feels like granite. I used to notice that once in a while Mary Lou, his sweet wife, seemed extremely tired. And I used to wonder why.

Sailing is one of Al's loves. He has owned several boats, and I'm talking 50- to 70-footers. He has always talked about building the ultimate sailboat, and he expects to get into one for something less than a quarter million bucks. Some day when he has the time, he likes to say, and has the cash, he adds … and Mary Lou groans.

One day Al spoke about his airplane, and I took the bait. "What airplane, I asked?"

"The one I used to own in Jakarta," he said coolly.

Humph. Sure, Al.

Poor Mary Lou started biting her lip, a sure sign that Al was about to spill the truth, sour as it might be.

Al had been an engineer for a petroleum company in Indonesia. He and a few other Americans (13 of them) gathered around a table in the Jakarta America Club and decided they needed an airplane. One of them said he could get an airplane without an engine. They could bring an engine into country through the embassy and get it all fixed up. Then they could all fly it as soon as they got their ratings. It reminded me of the 1920s comment by Herbert Hoover, who asked why he couldn't buy just one airplane and let all the pilots fly it.

One of the men in the group, an Air Force pilot, a colonel, would teach ground school. He was qualified. They would have to pay for books, which seemed reasonable, but they would end up with their single engine fixed-wing license! After all, that and a white scarf could make you the Red Barron on a good night in Jakarta!

At $800.00 each, it was a deal. They bought the airplane. Six months went by as the new engine was ordered, then three months as it was installed. Ground school was completed by all 13 owners and certified by the ground instructor. They were planning their first flight when, alas, the dastardly villain entered.

By deceit and treachery, the guy who brought the engine into country, a lower-level official of the not so sterling government, listed himself on the license for the aircraft as the owner. To spare you the whole stinky story, he took the freshly painted hot-pink aircraft, complete with new engine, and put it in his own hanger. It was found there with several other aircraft he had obtained by like deceit and treachery.

The 13 owners wandered around and found it easily (hot pink, remember!), and having never seen it before, they were taking turns sitting in it when the police came and ran them off. Al was delighted when he got to sit at the yoke and move all the controls. Anyway, the crook ended up paying back all the owners their investment plus 10%, so all was not lost.

Al never got his license, and he never did fly that airplane. But, he insisted, it was a great adventure! As he sat there with that twinkle in his eye, he whipped out an old white scarf and threw it around his neck. He struck a balding but elegant profile, and crowed, "How many folks can tell you they owned their own airplane … in Jakarta?"

Thoughts on High Standards

First, let's define "high standards." In the context of this article, standards are a set of values higher than the minimum at which society judges a person fit to continue to freely live his life. In other words, activities such as robbery, rape or murder require society to intervene with prison or discipline. Honesty, chastity, integrity and honor … well, society shrugs at the value of these virtues, and they are on the opposite end of this moral spectrum, where virtue is the norm and not the exception.

My daughter once asked what all those words meant, and I told her, "Having a husband or wife, and telling the truth." She seemed to understand perfectly. She didn't question the fringes, search for alternatives or nit-pick the details.

I have heard even good men say that it is difficult to live high standards. But it is just a matter of choice. And the world around us seems to scoff at the old standards of truth, virtue, chastity, honesty, integrity and honor. The word "righteous" these days is most often used to spit out some disparaging remark about someone who is supposed to be pretending to be "better" than the speaker. The context of good or faithful goals seems lost.

Years ago, I heard Vice President Dan Quayle mention that kids would be best served in their fight against AIDS (Auto Immune Deficiency Syndrome) if they learned abstinence from deviant or promiscuous sexual activity. The news media blasted him with words like naive and unrealistic. They portrayed him as incapable, the youthful vice president having been made to appear foolish again. Let's think about that just a minute.

Society today tells our youth that anything you want to do is okay, "as long as it doesn't hurt anyone else." (I take that to mean "get pregnant" or "get sick" or "kill someone.") We see the press and media portray risky lifestyles, such as drugs, sexual promiscuity and homosexuality as normal and healthy lifestyles. The schools teach much of this under the pretense that they are able to judge more properly than parents and do it much more effectively than family. I believe they teach some methods of consequence avoidance, but not social responsibility. It is done in a light that suggests only a conservative bumpkin could dampen our desire for this sort of activity. (And just who listens to conservative bumpkins?)

Our youth are told constantly that if a married couple wants to break up, it's just one of those things. Living together is a great way to see if marriage is right. Just file bankruptcy if you can't pay your debts. If you want a car, or new furniture or anything else, just get credit.

I don't buy it. Neither do the majority of Americans, no matter what the liberal press says.

This is what I think.

The old standards of truth, virtue, chastity, honesty, integrity and honor are critical to our survival as a nation. This old-fashioned stuff starts at home. It does not start at the daycare center, or in school.

Our children are not better educated by a public demonstration showing the placing of a prophylactic on a banana. The school may teach methodology, but it does not pretend to teach moral character. I think we are wrong. Popular opinion teaches that schools are qualified but that parents are stumbling, incompetent or worse. I think schools teach sex badly and cannot teach proper moral conduct at all.

The fact is that these days, promiscuity can kill you. Is that the only standard to which our society will respond? I will ensure my child gets some serious instruction before he uses a gun. As a parent, I have something important to say to my kids about sex. I don't need a banana and a prophylactic to do it, either.

The moral puzzle we have given our kids is displayed clearly here. A child cannot help but be confused by all the mixed signals. I still have a wonderful place for marriage at my house. Other things, such as financial responsibility, have to be taught from childhood, and I don't mean just addition and subtraction. Maybe the old work ethic we hear so much about should be tried on for size.

Let's call things what they are. Let's stop the half-truths we even say to ourselves— alternate lifestyle, pro-choice. When truth is unpleasant, society simply dresses it up and sells it as a thing more worthy. Is this the answer? Well, it is not my answer.

I admit it. I am old fashioned, cranky and hard to live with.

But I believe my children are getting honest answers, with more bite than society seems to want to give them.

On Taking a Stab at the Obvious

(Written sometime around 1990)

On Fort Rucker I met a very interesting captain who played the stock market. She was adept at sizing up the world and predicting the advance of certain market shares. For example, she foresaw the move from the once-popular nuclear sources (now we all wheeze when someone accuses us of ever believing in nuclear power) to more conventional power sources. She doesn't use much money, but she sure gets a lot of mileage out of her hobby.

Hey! I can do that. But instead of the market, I am going to share with you insight gained from years of experience as nothing special doing nothing in particular. We'll call this the First Annual Kingsley's Kranky Kalculations! Nostradamus, here I come.

First, I predict in the next decade, the medical profession will arrive at the point where, like it or not, the poor will get (what I call) Class C medical care; the middle class will get Class B care; the rich will get Class A care.

Oh, I see. You think this is awful, do you? The reality is that we do this to some degree already, because we all agree that it is worth $5,000, maybe even $500,000 of society's dollars to save a life. But is it worth $5 million to save that patient? Will the patient live a day? A week? A year? Will he/she die anyway? If the patient happens to have a million bucks, isn't it reasonable for the doctor to expect that he will more likely actually be paid for his services than if the patient has $4.23 in pocket change when they drag him in off the street? Or, if it is worth a million of society's dollars to save the life, how about $50 million? Okay, why not $50 billion? Yep. I think medicine will be great, but Class C medical care is here to stay.

Next, I also believe medicine will improve until men will live a very long time on average. The liberal media will pimp a liberal bent to the topic of suicide. And suicide will become the vogue method of leaving your family in old age. What a shame it will be for a man to refuse the bosom of a loving family in his most precious years.

President Clinton's honeymoon with NOW (National Organization of Women) and with the homosexual lobby will be short lived. Promised performance was what elected him. He made his bed with these folks on the premise that they would receive certain recognition from his administration. But as hard as he tries to please these people, he will never be able to do enough. In fact, I foresee that even congressmen and senators will have their backs against the wall on homosexuality and will finally make a public decision to support or not. I truly believe that many minority groups will finally speak out against the term minority being used to cloak gay rights groups in legitimacy.

This year (actually, in this presidency) congress will make another feeble effort to tackle the national debt, but while the debt may reel from the blows, it will promptly jump up and kick their butts. Over the next ten years, the older politicians will be voted out in anger over their lack of political will to do the job. The winds of popularity, controlled primarily by the image the press gives each issue, will blow back and forth across the entire spectrum of moral issues, and congress will flounder in despair. They may arrive at a point where they are incapable of forming a decision on anything. Men of courage and conviction will quit. Only men who enjoy torment, notoriety, public display of all they feel sacred, and humiliation to their families will tolerate the job.

A lot of information will come out about our new president's effort to become elected. For example: Even a blind man can feel his way around an elephant and figure out that it is a monster. But "I just didn't know how bad the debt was" and "The Bush administration was publishing optimistic figures" can be considered truthful only by the optimistic congressmen.

As more of our society becomes obsessed with "me, me, me," there will be a violent line drawn between the left and the right. Tolerance will become very limited. We see much of this already overseas. But it will happen more and more in the United States. Special interest group persecutions, especially churches and homosexual groups, will be on the increase this year. Every extremist will justify his activities with the actions of opposing extremists. Unless society adopts a higher moral ground, the peace we have always enjoyed could disappear as it has in South America.

Hand in hand with this, public services (cities, counties, states) will try desperately to establish the public image of integrity but will continue to suffer from severe corruption. (What a surprise, huh?)

Japan will decline and then vanish as an industrial power, simply because its major source of drive (the industry and thrift of her people) will become tainted by her success. Big challenges to the U.S. security and domination in the world will come primarily from warring little countries. One of them, in a terrorist mode, will obtain a nuclear device and use it. It is only a matter of time. But everyone in the world will be surprised, both by the act and by sudden awareness of whatever injustice will cause such an act. Then the nations will fail, unite and act.

I predict a cure or medicine to help AIDS patients. But another terrible, highly contagious venereal disease will take its place.

You doubt this? Okay. Now, by a show of hands.

Oh, I see. The doubters are the younger generation. Trust me. I say this because, even though some other terrible disease (non-venereal, such as a new or quickly killing cancer) may come along, the liberated part of society will consider medical advancement as absolute, and there will be unleashed new and unrestrained sexual activity, as happened in the 1960s. Without higher moral purpose as part of their reason for restraint, the exposure to new and more virulent strains of new (and even old) venereal diseases will become epidemic. Ask any doctor;

it is already epidemic. (I told you. This stuff doesn't take any rocket scientist.)

The mapping of chromosomes will become the most important and most controversial, medical achievement of the century. Coupled with the advancement of computer technology (which will be able to vastly increase speed over current super-computers), advancement in this research will be at blinding speed. Old diseases will be cured easily; symptoms we never really recognized before will become understood as medical problems and then cured. But this source of knowledge will create some of the most difficult moral questions yet asked by mankind.

For example: How long should an ordinary man be allowed to live? What is an acceptable quality of life? Who says so? Who has control over these technologies, and why? How much is a life worth, anyway?

Government will fall miserably short in its administration of these advances. Their effort to legislate morality will be hidden in rational arguments of things absolutely unrelated to moral thought. (The courts will even more severely discourage the application of moral standards to the logic of creating law than they do now.) The confusion of manmade legalities will be, in part, caused by the contradictory self-interest of different legislative and other offices of the government.

The only peaceful peoples in this great land will be those who know who they really are. They will generally have a great faith in a higher Being and have the moral courage to live according to their beliefs regardless of worldly wisdom.

I further predict that I am going to find a pizza I like better than a Baby Pan Pan with pepperoni and green olives. But I will gain 50 pounds if I do.

And Nutra System stock will soar this decade because of guys like me, who are always looking for a better pizza.

Chapter 6

Life on the Farm

Pitchfork I: On Choosing the Right Tool

When I was a boy growing up in Somerton, Arizona, I fancied myself to be vastly more skilled in the various arts of athletic competition than I really was, and I suffered significantly for my foolishness.

For example, I played football as a boy. I loved the sport, but I couldn't make the cut playing with my own year group of younger kids ("C Team"). I was bitterly disappointed when I discovered a wonderful secret. In the older group ("A Team"), there were so few big boys they welcomed another moving body, even a puny one such as mine. So I was happy to play. And I promptly broke my collarbone.

But nothing can compare to the abrupt learning curve gleaned from my experience with a pitchfork. It is the most deadly tool on the farm, as I discovered at about age ten. And rediscovered in high school.

MOBY DAD I: ADVENTURES IN LIVING

Every farm kid has done this, to one degree or another. But I had seen some pretty fancy pole-vaulting done with some successful flair. Even my little school had an old aluminum pole I had used to make a few modest leaps. And it only made me itch to try a real jump. I wanted to polish up, show Coach Moon I had some promise and use that pole in the pit. It was a real pit, with real sawdust and a fall-away bar. Maybe we could even get some kids to watch.

Anyway, I had to use something on my own to get up my experience level. I found an old broom handle lying around and tried to vault with that. But it was pretty short, and besides, it slipped each time I really tried to dig it in for the vault.

About that time I found the pitchfork. It looked pretty tall to me. I tried it, and it seemed to work pretty well. I tried it several times, in fact, and I got better each time. It was tall enough to get a fair vault, and it really dug in. And, as a bonus, it was just springy enough to let me imagine I could get a serious launch.

Now, my dad had built a fence around our front yard, about 40 inches high, I think. Four-by-four posts were planted 10 feet apart, on which rested two-by-fours. Wire was stretched around the outside, and it looked very neat. It kept the dog in, and more importantly, seemed like a reasonable goal for a ten-year-old, Olympic hopeful, pole vaulter.

Well, I got my faithful pitchfork, and I did the typical thing. I zeroed in on the only essential part of the mission I could think of in my excitement. I looked for that part of the fence with the softest landing zone on the other side. I ran up to the fence, and I launched.

It occurred to me later that I did not ponder several other important facts.

First, the ground on my side was especially soft.

Second, I did not consider that there were certain other mission-essential parts to the jump. These are listed in order of importance:

1. I had to get the altitude required.

2. If I couldn't get the perfect altitude, I had to at least clear the fence.

3. If I didn't clear the fence, certain precautions should be taken to protect my most delicate parts, even at the expense of broken bones.

I will never forget what happened next. I am sure it caused me to arrive two years late to puberty.

The fork dug in deep. This caused the handle to cease its assent about a third of the way up, but my ego insisted on trying to will myself over the fence.

I succeeded in getting only one leg up; and I landed squarely on the fence.

The pain was all consuming, to the exclusion of all else for a considerable time. I can only remember two other times I ever suffered the anguish I did at that moment. No humorous thoughts have ever crossed my mind to cover this moment in my life, probably because I can still remember being afraid I might be cursed to live through it.

The lesson now complete, I share it with you freely.

Beware the temptation to use a tool not designed for the job. Thinking ahead may well save you an enormous amount of grief.

Pitchfork II: My Experience on the Bar

As a freshman in high school I experienced a love affair with gymnastics. and I became thrilled with the gymnastics bar. I had a friend who was wonderful on it, and I envied his every feat. I was determined to learn some of those tricks.

One day I went home and began to look for a way to put up a bar of my very own. I had seen the bar at school up close, you know, and it didn't seem to require a rocket scientist to set one up. I finally found a bar I thought strong enough to do the job. It was an old pitchfork my Dad had lying around. It was smooth and without splinters. I quickly piled up a number of bales of hay in two piles and jammed the fork across the area between, about seven feet in the air.

Now, one of my friend's really intriguing tricks was that he could sit on the bar, then lean and flip forward all the way around the bar. I could only do it backward. Anyway, I determined to try his trick on my contraption.

No sooner was it up than I mounted the thing, grabbed it firmly, hooked my knees as well as I knew how, and leaned forward fiercely.

LIFE ON THE FARM

Wham!

I hit the dirt hard, face down, the bar having been wrenched from my hands by my own weight. I couldn't get my breath for a moment, and there was a very brief sensible thought that zipped through my mind. But it didn't stay long.

"Why hadn't I put down some loose hay, to soften—"

Just then, air was finally allowed into my lungs. Any rational thought left with the first breath of air. I was mad, now. Mad! Real mad! That dang thing, that low rent sucker wasn't going to get the best of me! Just a fluke that I happened to fall. I'll show that … that …

Before I even "thunk a real thought," I was back up on that thing. Grimy. Bloody. Teeth gritted. Determination was my sole functional thought. I grabbed the bar real hard, this time. I was going to flip around this sucker as though I were born to it!

Whop!

When I became aware, I was face down, struggling to get a precious gulp of air. I writhed in pain. The dust in my nose hurt badly, but I couldn't blow it out because nothing was working right in me.

My split lip, my bruised forehead, even my badly bleeding nose … nothing bothered me like the refusal of all that wonderful air to come into my face. The air just wasn't working. Or something wasn't. I mean, it had to be wonderful. And it had been there a moment ago, I was sure of it. Before this pain. But at this moment, it just didn't seem that I would ever get any of that precious air again.

And in a fleeting moment I vowed never, never to try the bar again, if only I could have a bite of that wonderful air.

My prayer was answered as I finally was able to gasp and get that wonderful air. It was full of burning dust and dirt. Lots of it. Seemed as though I could taste it. Only then did I realize I had a mouthful of dirt and no spit with which to eject it.

I lay there for 10 minutes, just to be sure the air, or my chest or something would still keep working.

I limped home in my torn and dirty clothes, cut, bruised and very unhappy. Mom asked me what happened, and I told her, "Nothing." But I made it clear that I was not trying out for the gymnastics team that year.

This was the second bad experience I had with a pitchfork. And to this day, every time I see an old pitchfork lying around, I remember clearly what it is for. Or rather, what it is not for. And if I have even a fleeting thought of using it for anything but hay, I immediately repent.

And I put it away.

Happiness Is What You Make It

I lived on one farm or another my whole childhood. I was particularly fond of animals, and tough chores with cattle or pigs were always secretly a joy to me. The animals on the farm had a definite pecking order. The stupidity of the cow, however, is exceeded only by two animals: the turkey and the chicken. And the lessons you can learn from stupid animals are universal.

LIFE ON THE FARM

I knew a Holstein (dairy) calf that was quite the center of attraction. She was cute and playful, and we all loved her. Calves always seemed brighter than cows to me, or at least cuter. But she was stupid like all the rest.

She started jumping her fence. At first, we thought this was clever. After all, the really dumb critters would aggravate Dad by leaning on the fence while reaching over it for greener grass, while she could sail over it.

But as she got older, and not much older either, this cute stunt became a real pain in the neck. We had to catch her at least weekly. Then daily. She would periodically aggravate our neighbor with her indiscriminate munching, but she was still cute.

Dad tired of her and finally sent her to auction. Frankly, we were grateful to see her go. She had papers, so it wasn't hard to sell her, but she wasn't any better for our neighbor down the road. She made it a real test, a battle of wills between her new owner and herself. Each fence got higher, and each successful leap brought new confidence that she could leap over the next one. Until a strange thing happened.

The calf became a cow. She was never content. The other side of the fence had greener grass, or the cattle in the next pasture had something she had to have. She simply could not be happy with her companions in her own pasture, with her own grass. She was very friendly and easy to catch, but she had to have her own way.

There came a day when Bossy weighed in at a little less than 1200 pounds and had an udder the size of a clothes basket. She was still gentle and almost fun to be around, but obstinate. She decided to get out of an enclosure where she was being treated for a minor disorder. Knowing she would want out, our neighbor made sure the fence was high and the gate was secure. She was fed more grain than usual, milked right on time and given fresh hay. She needed to be in there only two days, and she could have gone back to her pranks.

But nothing could please her. She just had to make the effort. If it had been any other fence on the place, she would have knocked it down. But this was a sturdy pen—heavy plank mounted on posts set in cement. It was nearly eight feet high. She got a running start and would have gotten at least a 7.5 for Olympic form.

She didn't quite make it, leaving part of her udder on that fence. She had to be destroyed.

Since this incident, I have paid close attention to my grandfather's commentary. He was an old dairy farmer who said really happy cows seem to feel the need to nose their fences, just to be sure they are hot (electrically charged). One good jolt a month seems to be almost comforting, and the happy cow, pleased with the knowledge of her limits, seems content to remain grazing in her own pasture. This is true. Ask any old farmer.

I believe kids are like that. Parents have to establish clear limits. Kids need to know their limits precisely, and they need to learn them while they are young. Then as they "nose the fence" (daily, it seems, during their teen years), they learn to be happy, grazing in their own pastures. It is true. Ask any old parent.

A kid is like a kite. The string (the limit) does not hold it back, but makes it soar.

The theory? If kids never try to scale the deadly fence, they will never destroy themselves on deadly limits.

The bottom line? They will learn to be truly happy.

Hey Mom and Dad, isn't that all we really want?

And All Through the House, Not Even a Mouse

Monday evenings in our home are reserved for the family. We try to make them fun and enlightening, some evenings being more serious than others. But the kids are always involved, and it usually turns into a good time.

One Monday during part of our family festivities, one of our cats caught a mouse, which caused a great stir among our children as she dragged it through our tiny trailer living room. She played with it a minute before Mom and Dad figured out what was going on and could act. But Nancy, our four-year-old, had seen it. She grew very upset and ran out of the living room crying.

I did the manly thing and snatched it up. I tossed it out with the cats and figured that was the end of that. But as the evening went on, I realized Nancy was no longer with us.

We stopped the festivities and fanned out to look for her everywhere. We found her outside, hiding. She was crying over that mouse. I didn't think much of it and went back into the house to resume our fun. But as I sat back down, I saw my sweet wife, Gail, enter at the other end of the room, a silent scream on her face.

She was pale, with a crazed look on her face intended to convey to me the advent of the world's end (as we know it), while desperately trying not to disturb the other children. Her frantic look was completed by her hands, which were rigid in front of her, fingers stiff and fully extended.

I looked at her in absolute bewilderment. I jumped up, prepared to fight lions and tigers, as though that might stop her obvious anguish.

"Pssst! Psssssst!" she hissed at me. She frantically motioned behind her toward Nancy, who was bashfully tip-toeing into the living room with one finger on her left hand stuck in her mouth, and tears washing a path through the dust on her face. Her little dungarees were dirty, her bare feet nearly black with the Alabama dust from a day of adventure. She wore a cut-off sweat shirt that framed her ruddy face and short curls, giving her a tiny "Tom Sawyer" look.

I was now even more confused and must have looked like an idiot to my wife, who was on the verge of letting that shriek out of her throat. She managed to mouth the word mouse before she had to close her eyes and choke off another urge to scream. She quivered a moment, then left the room.

I looked closely at Nancy and noticed that she had her right hand in her front pocket. Beside it, sticking straight up along the seam of her trousers, was a little mouse tail. I could hardly believe my eyes. I walked over and knelt beside her.

"Nancy," I asked quietly, "where is our mouse?" She looked around the room, her big eyes swelling with tears, not moving.

"Do you know where it is?" She started crying again, still not saying a word, chewing that finger like a stick of gum.

"Nancy, do you have that mouse in your pocket? Is that a little mouse-tail I see there?"

She burst into tears now, and came over to let me hold her. As I sat her on my knee, I looked over her shoulder into the kitchen. There, I could see my poor wife in the kitchen, wrestling with her disgust, trying desperately to let Dad handle it.

"Daddy," Nancy whispered tearfully. "Daddy, the kitties were hurting the mousy." She looked down at her pocket and patted it gently. There wasn't enough room in that pocket for a termite, much less her hand and a mouse. She looked at me and smiled.

"Nancy, that mouse is dead. There is nothing we could do about it, honey. It's okay, but you have to throw it outside now."

"Dad!" she insisted. "That mouse is okay. I have it right here." She patted it firmly now, as if I hadn't seen it before. "See?"

I patted her leg gently. I cupped her chin so she had to look at me, so that she would listen.

"Nancy, give me the mouse. It is dead and has been since before you got it."

I eased her off my knee and onto her feet. I managed to stand her up straight before I got hold of the mouse tail. She watched partly in anger, partly in disbelief, as I pulled the mouse out. It was nearly flat now, and she had no trouble seeing it was dead. Her face changed instantly.

"Well, okay, Dad! When do we get the ice cream?"

I thought my sweet wife would faint as Nancy wiped away her tears and ran into the next room to play.

On The Noble Pig, Part I: Tips on Owning a Pig

I am an animal lover, in a farmer sort of fashion. I mean, I cannot bear to see any animal suffer. In fact, I prefer to carry on a friendly relationship with it. My uncle would rather beat a cow than entice it to get into the milking stanchion, but it so much easier just to let it find fresh grain there. Nothing moves a cow like food.

On the other hand, I am practical enough to use every animal to its full talent. Horses provide a great way to ride and burn up spare money. Dogs are wonderful to herd animals, to keep watch and to keep you company. Cats chase mice and have kittens. But I prefer an honest animal and an up-front relationship. And thus, my love for the noble pig was born. The pig has three talents: test a good fence, dispose of table scraps and provide fresh bacon.

Oh, how I love pigs. If you have never raised them or had to do Dad's bidding in feeding the stock, you may not have the full appreciation for them I have. But I started raising pigs as a hobby, and in fact I kept my children busy with a few every year. As an addition to my dinner table, pigs were a very practical hobby. Army pay made them even more appreciated.

A pig is a very straight-forward, honest, animal. He is always hungry and happy to get food. He is faithful, preferring his pen-mates to any new-comer. He is generally smarter (and more stubborn) than a dog. He learns quickly to comply with the limits of his pen, but he keeps his owner honest, also. I have always said, "A fence isn't a fence until it has been tried by a hog." A shabby fence will not stand up to a serious pig of any size.

But in spite of all their attributes, there are a few basic rules you must remember in handling a pig.

First, you can't stop a pig, only turn him. A pig is shaped like a wedge, and you cannot stop one determined to go somewhere unless you already have a hold on him. If he is over 300 pounds, he won't even slow down. Don't try.

Second, it is a challenge to force a pig to do anything. A pig is easily turned and easily enticed and can then be fairly easily coaxed into going where he needs to be. With a little practice, even my family did fairly well with them. But just as

I am always careful with animals, I would never turn my back on a large pig. And I would never allow a child in a pig pen unsupervised.

Third, God put ears and tail on a pig so it can be coaxed in those vexing moments when it cannot be enticed. Use them.

Fourth, if you give a pig space, clean water and clean food, it will grow and be happy without all the stink credited to it. We kept them in several roomy pens so they were able to root or have clean feed easily. Pigs are clean and will remain so if not crowded by economy-minded farmers. I suppose a thousand hogs in my pen might have changed my resolve to have them.

Fifth, if you intend to make a pig useful, you must plan ahead. Set up the fence in the vicinity of any brushy area you need cleaned (down to the depth of the topsoil). If you leave the pen there long enough, all living growth will be gone. If you have six or so kids and have any table scraps, a pig will make short work of them and will return some good wasted food to your table in the form of pork. If you have a cow, pigs will dispose of the spare milk. If you have sour milk, they like it even better, for they have a natural need for the bacteria in sour food. If you plan carefully and place the pen (with one or two pigs) on a route into your property, they are excellent watch-pigs, woofing and snorting at any newcomer.

Last, if you intend to eat your pig—and we all do unless we are like some of the more foolish wealthy—raise them in pairs (or more) and refuse to name them. Kept this way, they are less social and seem to be less friendly to loving children. (This also makes it less likely that you will find your kid rolling around the pen, playing with your pig and in serious need of personal hygiene.)

Naturally, a pig is a lot easier to eat when it isn't called Tammy or Oscar or some other mushy name. We'll talk about this next.

On The Noble Pig, Part II: You Can't Eat a Pork Chop Named Joey!

My start in raising hogs occurred with a friend who assured me he would get us started. We kept our prize porker in a little electric-fence pen. Joey, we called him. He became almost a family pet, the smartest animal I think I ever saw. Smarter than the average dog. He was certainly smarter than I was.

When we first picked up our pig, we helped our friend "nose-ring" all his piglets, along with Joey. It was an interesting operation, designed to accomplish two things. First, a nose ring will prevent pigs from razing all living things in the pen and creating great holes. Second, that little metal ring allows excellent contact with the electric fence, and a pig's boundary learning-curve is greatly improved.

I hate to admit it, but I had a learning curve of my own enhanced by pigs on several occasions.

First, as we were nose-ringing those piglets, one got away. He jumped the four-foot side of the stake-bed truck, and down the road he went. We spent eight hours chasing that pig around 60 acres of land. Let the good times roll.

Since that day, I have sworn to keep a gun out where I was ringing pigs. If a pig gets away from me, he'll either be dead before he gets over the horizon, or he will run until I won't have to worry about him anymore.

Next, I had heard the quickest way to break a pig to the fence is to pick up his back legs and steer his nose onto the fence. He will yelp, but he will not forget. Thus is born a field-expedient, but effective, lesson in boundaries.

Well, on the day appointed for Joey's lesson, it had rained hard the night before. Morning came with everything in the universe water-logged. I dutifully picked up the soaking wet back legs of my pig, and connected his nose to the fence.

A funny thing happened. I became an integral part of the circuit and was struck by the bolt of electricity as it seemed to pass up my pig entirely. And I became inspired in my own right.

Then, without our knowledge, our electric fencer broke. No electricity was applied to the fence for what we estimated to be nearly a month. Joey got out and learned he could root at will in some sweet clover. He was never afraid of the fence after that. He would just run over it whenever he wanted. My wife would have the kids round him up and set out a little sour milk in the pen. Then they would have to stand out of the way as he ran back to the pen to get it.

The summer we had him, it was awfully hot, and we had to water Joey down twice a day. Before it was over, Joey would prance and tease to be sprayed with water, would play with my children as he was fed, and would purr (groan) if you rubbed him behind the ears.

Joey was also a terrific watch-pig. He would woof and snort if anyone came within a half mile of our house. He had several distinctive types of woofs, which would let us know when he was scared, curious, hungry or mad. And his message was clear to all who knew him.

Anyway, the big day came for Joey to be converted to sausage. My friend came over to load him into his stock trailer. He was a peaceful but practical man who came with the philosophy that three big, ugly guys (the bigger and uglier, the better) could grab a pig and make it do anything. That worked well enough, and soon Joey was loaded.

Now this, my first pig, is the reason I don't name my pigs anymore. We all knew he would end up in the freezer, so it was not unexpected. Just the same, it was tough for me to bridge the gap for my kids between Joey's disappearance and fresh pork on the table. In my usual evasive teaching-discussion, I approached the children with a vague sentence starting with something like, "Bye-bye, Joey," and ending up with something like, "Wow! Look at Mom's pork chops!"

It worked.

Today, Joey still holds an honored place in our family. Sort of a "Pigs Hall of Fame" in our family history. He is revered even by the children who can't remember him. But I learned my most valuable pig-lesson from him.

It's hard to eat a pork chop named Joey.

On The Noble Pig, Part III: Continuing Chronicles of a Fledgling Pig Farmer

We learned quite a lot from our first pig, but we learned a different set of lessons from the second batch of pigs we raised. We did well enough raising them on our own, but when the time came to load them up, my farmer-friend had hurt his back, and thus was unable to participate in our effort. Because I had come to depend on his assistance, the surprise was as demoralizing as it was inconvenient.

Since he felt so bad, my friend arranged for his son to drop the trailer off at our place. As he pulled in, I went out to help him load my pigs. But as he finished unhitching the trailer, he turned to me and said, with a smile, "Bye-bye! We'll be back for it in the morning!"

I think there was a conciliatory mention of luck thrown in for good measure. But that kid was no dummy, and he hated loading pigs. So with that, reality fell upon me like a block of wood.

LIFE ON THE FARM

I was feeling sort of droopy as I trudged into the house. Maybe confused is a better word. I wasn't really up on the skill set related to the chasing and catching of pigs, and I had been only a hapless participant by default in the last loading. This time was different for three reasons.

First, we were missing the three big ugly guys to capture and handle the pigs.

Second, there were two pigs this time, and they were not nearly as friendly and cooperative as the first pig had been.

Third, the experience had just driven away, and I could not hope for assistance to smooth out my education in this effort.

There was nothing left to do except to do it! Might as well put on a positive face, I thought to myself. Besides, Mama was watching through a window, and I know how good she feels when I pretend to know what I'm doing. Even when I don't, that seems to be half the requirement for success! I puffed myself up and strutted into the house.

"Men," I addressed my sons, ages nine and 11. "We have a job to do. Get on your old clothes. Meet me in the pen."

We met in the yard outside the pen and talked in a whisper, so the pigs couldn't hear and figure out our plan. We discussed our options in detail. After all, these boys were seasoned veterans from Pig Number 1, and they had to be let in on the whole discussion so they could participate in the solution.

"Well, maybe we should do it like before," one of the boys suggested.

I was miffed. "You mean, you guys will talk about holding the tail while you expect Dad to toss the porker into the trailer, right?" I jabbed.

"Oh no, Dad." Donny shook his head sincerely. "We'll chase them, honest! All you have to do is catch them!"

That did it. I started hatching hare-brained ideas faster than popcorn kernels going off in a popper.

Okay, I decided, we'll entice the pigs into the trailer with food.

Nope. Those pigs would not cross the electric fence even after we took it down.

How about driving them out the gate and into the trailer?

Nope again. No self-respecting pig ever goes where he should, and the trailer was nearly enroute to the sweetest-rooting 13 acres a hungry pig ever saw.

Anyway, time being critical, the "big, mean and ugly approach" to pig loading (see previous section) began to seem acceptable to me. By default, you can always be mean and ugly when you don't have time to kind and sweet. We rolled up our sleeves and made our plans.

I had read in a book that with a bucket over a pig's head, he would back up just anywhere you wanted. So Jeffrey had his bucket at the ready.

Aspiring pig farmers, beware! There is a lot to be said for a Sumo Wrestler being the effective operator of this bucket. A

60-pound kid does not do well wrestling a 200-pound pig, even with a bucket.

Anyway, we put out a little sour milk, slinked up behind the porkers, and made a grab! Missed! Then the chase.

First one direction. Then another. Still no luck. Then, a lull in the action, and we all stood quietly a moment, eying the pigs and breathing heavily. My boys needed a boost!

"We have those pigs on the ropes, men! They're really tired," I declared, in an attempt to encourage my weary troops. They were not convinced.

Suddenly Jeff had them cornered, and as the little pig ran by, I grabbed a leg. Why, before I knew it, that sucker was kicking tar out of me! Holy cow, it was tough holding onto that pig! I felt like a 200-pound man was beating me up! Jeffrey kept trying to put the bucket over his head, Donny kept trying to help, the pig kept turning in circles, and I was just hanging on!

Donny eventually gave up and left Jeff and me to fight the battle.

I finally got the pig onto his back, and started to "hog tie" him, when I heard a very shaky voice behind me yell.

"I've got him! I've got him!!" It was Donny, my nine-year old.

Then Jeff yelled, "I'm coming Donny!" And suddenly I was alone. Alone. With a wildly thrashing, uncooperative hog.

I glanced up to see Donny hanging on to the other pig for dear life. He was astraddle his neck backwards, holding a grain bag over his head, being bounced up and down in the air as the pig ran back and forth the length of our pen.

I quickly tied off my hog and turned to help the boys. Jeff had the pig's tail and was digging in, trying with all his might to slow that pig down … to no avail.

"Dad! We got him!" Jeff yelled. Who has who, I wondered. I leaped into the fray and grabbed the pig's legs.

Around and around we went, the choking dust now so thick we couldn't see more than 10 feet. It was growing darker by the minute, but each lap around the pen was closer to the trailer-end. Finally, having worn the pig down, I grabbed the rear legs, each boy grabbed a front leg, and we heaved porky into the trailer.

Whew. One in, one more to go.

We stood there in the near-dark, breathing heavily in the choking dust, filthy and exhausted. My younger assistant pled with me to get help. He was absolutely exhausted. Heck, I was absolutely exhausted. I made a command decision.

Time for the cavalry. I sent my son in to call our friend for help.

My oldest son and I trudged back into the pen to prepare ourselves for one more major effort. He was tired but did not complain—not a single whisper. Only determination showed on his face. The pig I had tied off stood defiantly at the far end of the pen, the rope still securely tied only to his forward hock. We squared off and thought bad things about each other.

I picked up my end of the rope and was contemplating the wrestling match about to ensue when in an instant we were delivered from this stressful moment. I looked at the rope in my hands, stared at the pig, and suddenly realized that a pig on three legs is an immovable pig. Victory was ours.

We began to coax the pig toward the trailer, and when he fought it, I simply tugged on that rope and lifted that leg off the ground. He would immediately quiet down, and we would resume the effort. In no time at all, the pig was loaded.

We were exhausted, but I was happy. My farmer friend arrived too late to help, too polite to comment on the way we smelled, and too smart to laugh out loud. My oldest son, something obviously on his mind, paid him no mind. He prowled around the tailgate and eye-balled the lock and the pigs.

"Get them in the freezer, Dad." he grumbled. "I've had all the fun I can stand with these guys."

Mother's Knee

What a man learns to love and desire begins in the home. The cure to many of society's ills are found at Mother's knee. Congress would be wise indeed to invest in 10 million or so pairs of Mothers' knees!

And For These Blessings

In early November one year, our dog, Andy, disappeared. His was a quiet presence. You know how it is around a country place. When there was fishing or camping, Andy was always there, but otherwise, all he ever did worthy of mention was chase away cows rummaging around our corn patch.

My kids had always taken him for granted, but now he was sorely missed. Every mealtime as our faithful mutt failed to return, concern grew. He had never been gone overnight before, so this was rather unusual. We had recently chased off several groups of wild dogs and suspected Andy may have wandered off with them, which worried us even more.

I preparing to take a shower early around 9 A.M. one Saturday when it happened.

"Aarrghhhh!"

It was the kind of guttural groan that makes your heart stop, shrieked from the kitchen by a wretched soul. It was my sweet son, desperate to lend his help to some terrible situation he could not fully understand. It brought to mind the biblical discussion of wailing and gnashing of teeth, and the "fight or run instinct" took over in me. I leaped out of the bathroom, nearly unclad.

"He's lost his foot! Aarrghhhh!"

My blood froze. Kids, not all mine, were outside. And tools—like axes, saws and plows. There were yearling bulls, cows, horses and things that could easily snuff out the tender life of a kid being silly or stupid.

I ripped an Army webbed belt out of my uniform, the kind with the slip lock buckle that would allow me to cinch down a tourniquet … should I need it… for the kid I could see in my mind's eye, helpless outside.

I raced outside to see my daughter, Nancy. She was holding our faithful dog, Andy, by the collar, touching his head gently. The rest of the kids were standing around in one state of mourning or another. Nancy was crying, trying not to look at Andy's foot. She was prancing around as though her spirit wanted to fly away, but her body just couldn't go along. I took the collar and sent her in the house.

"Daddy, is Andy going to die?" Her big eyes swelled with tears.

"Yes," I said firmly.

We had animals. Animals die. We even have to destroy them on occasion. She knew this. Tears streamed from her face as she went into the house, and her brother Donny came outside again.

"Dad, should we pray for Andy?" he asked.

"Yes." I nodded grimly.

I knew we had to end this quickly. I could see that the missing foot had been gone for at least two days, and the dog was suffering.

"Tell all the kids to pray for Andy. Call Jeff out here. Tell him to bring the gun."

Donny shrieked again. There was a look of horror, of terrible pain and disbelief that I will never forget. He bolted into the house and screamed for his mother.

My sweet wife, having more kid-savvy than I, came out and wordlessly took my arm. I was wired for high tension at the moment, and she knew exactly how to read me, as she always does. She waited for the right moment, and she started.

She had called around and found a vet in town, and he was waiting for me. She convinced me to take the dog in and have him put to sleep. She was gentle, but persuasive.

"Do you want anyone living here to still call you Dad?"

So my oldest son and I loaded Andy into the truck, and off we went to find the vet who would do this on a Saturday. He was very kind.

"The dog isn't too bad," he said, "and, I just might save him ..." for a mere $250.

I'm kind of wimpy. After all, I really did still want to be the dad. It would certainly be questionable after this. That was a lot of money back then. But that did not matter. I called Mom and got the okay if the vet would take plastic money.

All seemed well for a few days. Then came infection and Doggie Intensive Care. The bill came to over $400.00. That was an especially healthy chunk of change, especially back then. But you just couldn't take the dog back and demand a refund. And I was much more likely to be voted Dad of the Year should there ever be such a tally in my house.

Well, we still have our wonderful dog, and I am still the wonderful dad. He can still chase those cows, but he is a bit more subdued than he used to be. Nancy gets mad at me every time I call him Tripod, but she still loves me.

And this holiday season wouldn't be complete without a footnote of the wonder it has brought to our house.

Over Thanksgiving dinner, as Nancy blessed the food, she called to mind our beloved dog with wonderful words only a child can whisper. She gave heartfelt thanks. And as she wrestled with the Lord over our many blessings, Nancy humbled all of us with her faithful plea.

"And God, won't you please hurry up and grow his leg back."

MOBY DAD I: ADVENTURES IN LIVING

.

Chapter 7

Noble Thoughts

Wanted: Hero. No Experience Necessary

Have you ever noticed how the only rotten kids always live down the street? I mean, you're kid … my kid … they are learning, having problems, working them out. It is all part of growing up, gaining maturity. But the kid down the street, he's a rotten kid.

Well, pal, here's a flash for you. There aren't any rotten kids. Every kid labeled a loser is one by virtue of the fact that he has never experienced winning. Ethnic background may limit opportunities, but it cannot defeat a winning attitude. Winning is a key part of being a success, and I think every kid has to be taught the essential elements of winning. Or he may never be a winner.

I was raised in a dysfunctional home where I was never quite sure who I was or what I was, or what was real. Alcohol was the primary culprit.

Whatever I did right while growing up was caused by the channeling of my confusion by a select few wonderful people. The town librarian taught me to explore my world; a sweet old woman taught me the dignity of age; my first faithful, grouchy old boss taught me work ethic and self-respect; and I learned further from several "adopted" dads and moms, several specific

**1991 Michael & Donny Kingsley
with Donny's Math Trophy**

teachers and many others. Most did nothing big. They taught me little things, all of which changed my life.

The names of these wonderful people are not exactly household words: Mrs. Shipp, the librarian; Bob Russell, the employer; Don and Dorothy Donald; Mom and Dad Peterson; Mom and Dad Fancher; Dick Tierney; Grandma Kuster; Uncle Charles; Auntie Sues and Uncle George; Bob Moody; Jim and Linda; Margaret Manus. There were others, but I know many other boys (now men) who owe them the same debt I do. Many. And there were girls who owe them, too. There may be hundreds of them. Can you imagine that? Kids who needed someone, some word of encouragement—something not from Mom or Dad.

Once, one of my sons had a really hard time adjusting to his new school. He wore very heavy glasses and was branded a nerd. At age 12 it doesn't take anything else.

He got into a time when he was really clumsy. He was growing faster than he could keep control of some of his far distant appendages. Anyway, he joined a math club. This was a nerd thing to do, but he loved it so much he started telling math jokes.

He worked at it. He started staying late after school, where some poor schmuck coached him and a half dozen other kids in the finer points of math competition. And he was pretty good.

One day he went away and won first place in a three-state contest. He brought home a trophy four feet tall. It seemed then as though those four feet were added directly to his stature.

The trophy was so big he had to lay it across the laps of two other kids to get it and himself into the car. Happy does not describe a reformed nerd lugging in a piece of hardware bigger than he is! And Mr. Myers, my son's math teacher, the schmuck who worked night after night coaching those kids—God Bless Mr. Myers—stood back quietly, out of the light, and bragged about my son. He became a different boy.

This principle, this effort to help a youth in need of guidance, is called "mentoring." Sometimes, even a perfect mom and dad cannot reach a kid whose good sense has fallen prey to puberty or peer pressure. But he can be saved by someone. Maybe you are that someone.

All successful men and women have had a mentor. It is easy to do, and we each must do it. Somehow, you are uniquely positioned to reach down and mentor some kid. He may be five or 25. You may be rich or poor, big or small, love or hate kids. You may be the football coach or an elderly widow. You may have to pay a price to do it. But some kid needs your help and will love you forever for throwing him a line.

Next time you see a rotten kid with a really bad attitude, remember there is a little sign tattooed on his heart, which even he cannot see: "Wanted: Hero. No Experience Necessary."

Our Debt

In some nations, a man is doing well if he provides a place for his family to sleep and enough food to keep the kids from crying. In the United States, we have the privilege to complain if we're out of Frosted Flakes, or if the pop is too warm.

This privilege was purchased by another generation. It is our turn to pick up the tab.

Failure

More often than not, failure in life come from lack of attempt. Fear, lack of conviction—there are a lot of distracters. But taking the first step is the most important.

Patriotism

Nothing stirs my heart like the patriotic story of a hero who strives, sacrifices and prevails against heavy odds. Because of this, I used to fear that I loved war. This is against all I really do appreciate.

It is not so.

I hate war.

But I do love the noble struggle.

Mom

The world seems to measure a man by a moment of performance. Once a hero, once in the spotlight, it is an image that seems to stick.

I doubt that it is the moment of courage displayed on the battlefield or during the moment of terrifying crisis that is the real measure of the man. I believe, rather, it is the years of preparation, the years of shaping the attitude and deep-felt values. These prepare a man to call forth that courageous and instantaneous decision without hesitation. This should be heralded as the real measure of that courage.

I am convinced this is true. I heard the tape recording of a pilot trying desperately to get a large airliner down over a big city after he had been hit by another aircraft. As they approached the ground, upright only by his great skill and, certainly, without a chance of survival, he calmly told his copilot: "Okay, Jack, tell 'em all to brace back there."

His courage was learned long before the crisis.

A friend of mine, a jolly old fat guy who is full of life and cannot be brought to dismay, began to describe his march up Bataan to meet the Japanese, then the battle back down until capture, then the march north again in captivity.

He didn't begin to cry until his description of prisoner life aboard ship. He was sent on the first ship of prisoners to prison camp in Japan. He remained in captivity for the duration of the war. He felt terribly guilty for surviving that ordeal. No one knew this guy as I did, and few knew of the iron courage he kept quietly inside.

And so my own feeble efforts pale by comparison to this great man.

I have had my own trials. Well, at least one which stands out. I've referred to it in two previous chapters. It was not in battle, but in a crisis. I, however, had no option. I risked it all without a second thought, playing the odds, going exactly by the book under immense pressure. But I had no choice. The only options were to die or go down fighting. I would have done anything to have avoided the moment, including cowardice. But there I was, in a pickle, and I had only one chance. I did it right, and I got lucky. I survived.

Another man was with me. We did not particularly care for each other. But he was so grateful to survive, that suddenly to him I was the miracle man of the unit. He became the architect of my new, heroic image.

But I was hardly able to swallow afterwards. I was barely able to walk on my shaking legs, and I went back to my tent immediately so no one could see how scared I really was. I felt so ashamed of my terror that I wanted only to be alone.

My fear was so traumatic that in those initial few hours alone, I began to blame myself for the emergency. I had so many doubts about what had really happened. Was it actually my fault? Had I checked everything? Had I done all I should have? Was I guilty of failing to do something important?

When I was called out for a meeting that evening, I was still so strung out that when a great man reached out his hand to congratulate me, I nearly spit in his eye. I thought he was making fun of my fear. But it was true, I had done well, and that 30 seconds had made me the local (undeserving) hero.

As I think about that moment, I should have done well. I mean, I had a wonderful role model who rivals any I have ever seen. Courage, integrity, patience, faithful support, and yes, love were all taught in a sterling fashion. When I joined the Marine Corps years earlier, no one was more ready to carry the flag for me. When I joined the Army, years later, all nay-sayers had to put up with my mentor.

I am a lucky man. If I had broken that helicopter after she, my mentor, had put me back together, she would have been mad at me for not pulling it off.

You see, my mom just won't take no for an answer. And whatever courage I ever claim will be from the years she invested in me. Not the Marine Corps. Not the Army. Mom.

Thanks, Mom.

Fidelity

Nothing speaks peace to the soul of a man like the laughter of his wife and children. Happy children are the measure of the condition of his inner spirit. His real feelings toward his sweet wife are mirrored by the adoration his children feel for the two parents.

The loving mother provides the milk of human kindness from which the child drinks all his life. It shapes his basic goodness and satisfies his thirst for knowledge and understanding.

The faithful and loving husband creates the opportunity for a child to learn his real identity. From Dad, the child becomes confident of his real direction, and he strives to become all he can be. From Dad's example, the child begins to understand his/her responsibility to generations yet unborn.

A parent who decides to go a separate direction, as with divorce or infidelity, destroys so very much more than the simple union of two people. Generations are damaged. Nations are weakened. Humanity is diminished.

What Price Character?

Do you want to measure the real depth of a man's character? Spend an evening watching him with his children. Spend another watching him away from his wife. Offer him an opportunity to do a professional courtesy for a man not a friend or an enemy to him.

We all complain because no one has it anymore, but real character costs more than many men are willing to pay.

Homage

This was written 28 January 1986, while I was the safety officer on the United States Precision Helicopter Team.

The space shuttle blew up today. The whole world, and especially all airmen, mourn the loss of those souls.

I was filing a flight plan when someone yelled that the shuttle had blown up. On a television monitor, I saw the newsman's confusion over what had happened. He could not see the monitor, which made what had happened obvious as they played it back and talked of possible survivors.

I watched the shuttle evaporate during the replay and cursed the feeble nature of men whose only genuine, lasting quality is their fearless pursuit of lofty goals in the face of incredible odds.

God bless them. I hope somehow the esteem we feel for that crew makes a difference in the merit with which their lives on this earth are judged.

Let a Man Hunger

A child who wants for nothing eventually seeks for nothing more than entertainment. Base desires without discipline lead a man to the gutter.

Let a man hunger for freedom, justice, knowledge, love or any of life's higher ambitions, and he will move mountains.

Voice of the People

In an election year such as 1992, when the political tapioca is hitting the fan, with all the politicians licking their lips and circling for the kill, I have noticed a terrible trend. Worse than apathy, it is more deceitfully employed than propaganda. I can only describe it as social shock. Think about it.

Only one third of the registered voters turned out for the New York primary. I believe this is caused in no small part by the media and their numbing saturation of the average man with tragedy in the very extreme.

We cause this to some degree as a society, and I can accept my share of the blame. I mean, we all crab and complain until we make an art form of it. But the media have become obsessed with the sensationalism required for big ratings and have used it to whip the public into hysteria over one issue or another.

In the end, the horrid has become commonplace; the unimaginable is widely, publicly discussed and even expected, right down to the methods, the purpose and the motives (even the interviews) of the (cheerful) perpetrators of horrid crimes.

Okay, moral issues belong to another chapter. I am addressing how the desperate search for sensational news has clouded objective reporting of all political candidates, and how it has discouraged the average man from his duty. What is at stake is nothing less than our ability to exercise control over our nation, and we must wake up to what is happening around us.

This bombardment of the press creates what I call "invincible apathy." All the presidential and state office candidates, every one of them better men than I, are portrayed as idiots at worst, and without any respect for their position at best. Perhaps I am an idiot, but I would (have, actually) stand in awe in the presence of the President of the United States, or even the governor of our state.

There is no respect anymore. And gloom is the key point of every report on politically significant events. Unspoken, the message seems to be "So, why vote?"

It is an insidious thought, one which creeps unspoken into almost every political and news broadcast I see. One idiot is as good as another, isn't (s)he? Talk about depressing! We used to look at the distance between stars to perhaps relate to incredible numbers; now we look at the mounting national debt. It all seems so hopeless. The savings and loan scandal is not even mentioned anymore, even by the media, perhaps because it is too terrible, too devastating, too difficult.

We have an old joke in aviation that applies here. It is said that in event of an engine failure at night, when you don't like what you see with your landing light, just turn the darn thing off. Sort of like the guy who, when he learned how dangerous smoking was, decided to stop reading.

The president will be re-elected anyway, won't he? If congresspersons are all idiots or worse, by default, our next president is bound to be a check-bouncing, favor-seeking jerk. Don't you think so? The governor will keep abusing his airplane, whether or not the rest of us know about it, right? The mayor is still going to try stuff I don't like, but I can make no difference. You vote. You go to the town meeting. I have better things to do.

The crowning touch for me happened today. It was the surrender of hope as I see it. A radio man said the state of Kansas is considering not having a primary election. Maybe they weren't serious, but the newsman made it clear that it would save millions of dollars, and that Kansas doesn't command enough delegates to influence the outcome.

Well, it follows that this is nearly as true for Alabama. How about Oklahoma? Arizona? Florida? Pick a state. Your state! We are only a tiny part of the picture, whatever state we're from.

Where are we going with this? Should we throw down the flag and quit?

Think of all those Tuesdays we could free up. Or maybe we should just let our state legislature make our choices for us. Or better yet, we'll get Dan Rather, Merv Griffin, Nina Totenburg, Oprah and some of the others to select our president, our governor, our congressmen. Then they can take exit polls from each other and let us know what we decided.

I believe we will all be held accountable for our apathy. We will become all we detest unless we act. We have no excuse for our inaction.

Get mad, America. No one can beat us. Let's not beat ourselves.

Vote.

Choosing Right and Wrong

I believe the real truth in any organization, the genuine reason for its existence and the validity of that existence are easily discernible to any pure heart. As I have traveled this nation and visited clubs, churches and businesses, I have found this principle seems to apply in every case.

It remains for me to maintain a pure and unbiased heart. I believe Christian ethics and beliefs are not given to us just so we can be obedient by knowing God's will. They bring to us the gift of discernment of good and evil, as well, if we practice our beliefs.

I also believe we are accountable for that gift.

Gift of a Friend

In an awful moment of despair, a friend has the gift to pull you through. It is the gift of hope.

A friend can listen to all the grief you can muster, sift through it to pick out the golden nuggets of truth, throw away the trash and offer you his love and strength. He can give you a perspective of your own goodness and restore your view that the world can be made better.

Only in America

Only in America can a man without a job be 80 pounds overweight, complain about standing in line to register for his unemployment benefits and then have enough political clout to defeat a congressional bill requiring him to render service for his welfare check.

A smart politician will figure out a way to care for the needy and put the lazy back to work. Till then, I suppose it's still a pretty good system.

Treasures Laid Up In Heaven

There is a side to humanity you cannot appreciate until you've played Santa Claus to a sweet child whose father can't rub two nickels together, but out of gratitude would make you wealthy, were it in his power.

Is this not part of the "treasures laid up in heaven"?

Example

The most difficult burden a man bears in this life is the mold into which he attempts to pour his son.

Mom Is a Hero

Not all the things we remember are good or fun. I believe some things don't even have an appropriate place in this public forum. And I am not sure this article belongs here, but some of you will be able to relate to this, and you may need to share the same thought.

My mom is a hero.

I was raised in a home where I thought things were real—as they really were all over. I believed the things told to me by my father, that somehow he was superior to the balance of the universe, and that there was another reason for every problem, every failure.

I oversimplify here, because not only was he a basically good man, but he was usually honest, in the socially acceptable standard of honesty. He worked like a draft horse, and he loved his children as well as he was capable.

However, his behavior was all part of the strange workings of someone completely dysfunctional—an alcoholic incapable of knowing or teaching reality. His entire life, it seems in retrospect, was spent in regret or anger over one part of his fate or another. When I was a boy, Dad convinced me Mom was a major part of his failings in life. He would, on one hand, become angry about my disagreements with Mom, but on the other, would stir the pot to ensure our mutual animosity. In the end, he left the family and died young, alone and miserable.

So I was raised by a hero. Mom was brought up in the old school, where mothers stayed home and raised kids. She had to break that mold when the money got so very tight she needed to keep the books for my dad's business. But he was completely unable to realize the value of her guidance and was very abusive, especially about the work she did. So she quit and got another job.

She became an excellent bookkeeper and got an even better job. Dad's business went broke. She continued to work.

Drinking steadily, Dad spent 18 months trying to invent something that was supposed to make us rich. He stopped looking for work, but Mom hung on. He was abusive to all of us, either physically or mentally. And Mom became the buffer.

And what did I do to help her pull the load, to deal with these terrible problems? Nothing. Heck, I didn't have a clue. I had all the answers. She was just a mean woman, and I was certain my unhappiness and most of Dad's could be laid to her. I held a job; I funneled money into the family and bought my clothes and books and had my own money. But I blamed my problems on Mom.

I was so very young and foolish, and so very wrong.

What do real heroes do? She did all of that and more. She cheered for me. She protected me when she could. She took blame for my shortcomings. She hollered at me for joining the Marine Corps, but she met me at the plane on my first leave, waving a little flag. She encouraged and harassed me until I started making smart decisions. She never doubted I would make it in the world. She endured to the end.

She stayed married until she had no options, probably longer than any other hero could have stood it; then she started over—alone, broke, with a daughter still at home. She got another job, re-established herself as a great bookkeeper and got her last child through college. She found a good man, and after some serious persuasion, married. Heck, he and I get along better than he and she, so you know he's okay. And I think now, she will be okay, too. No thanks to me.

I love my mom. It is not one of those mushy kinds of "mommy" things. She is a tough old bird. And Mom is just as tough now as ever. At least that's the image she puts on for all to see. But I married someone a lot like her, so I see through that better than I used to.

My mom is a hero. We need more of them.

The Gem

A raw diamond represents an incredible potential. Each stroke of the mallet will either bring forth a new and brilliant facet or shatter the stone and render it a fraction of its former potential value.

The craftsman in whose trust the stone is placed is experienced. He knows the stone with an expert eye, and he waits all his life to work on a real masterpiece. Given this wonderful opportunity, he will weigh the merits of each stroke over and over before taking the swing.

His good name will be made or broken by the success of his effort.

A child is born with unlimited potential. The young mother must shape his character with gentle firmness, instill a set of values and teach him to realize his potential. The mother in whose trust the child is placed knows the child better than all the world and, thus, his potential. She has waited all her life to work on this masterpiece, and she knows each stroke must be placed to bring out every facet of his character. An improper blow may ruin her masterpiece. She will spend her life weighing the merits of each decision required for his welfare.

Her heart shall be made or broken by the success of her effort.

How Sweet the Name Mother

How sweet is the name Mother—sung by good men who have had a loving and caring one, and taken in vain to describe the sons who didn't.

How much misery would be channeled into good and righteous paths if a mother's love could be required for the birth of each child.

Noble Thoughts

Noble thoughts are a burden to the bearer.

Not often a terrible burden, mind you. Sort of like a baby, a cherished loving child who needs to be carried or coached all along the path of life. A child who is loved will grow, do well and be a joy forever. One that is not loved will withdraw, wither and die. This is true, as well, of a noble thought.

I believe every man is born with noble thoughts, but the average man prunes his thoughts until he keeps only the thoughts his heart can stand. A noble thought to a man who is not able to bear it is like a glowing coal contained in the bottom of a paper cup. It will soon be gone and forgotten.

I believe society has so perverted noble thought that there is little of it left. Brazen foolishness has become mistaken for bravery, and such behavior, if conducted for a "suitable reason" is regarded as acceptable by the public at large.

The tender feelings between a father and a child have become the tear-jerking backdrop of a commercial for a hamburger chain. Sacred love between a man and a woman is displayed as animal lust in the context of an illicit relationship. The creation of life is portrayed as a dastardly blow to the would-be liberated woman, her further enslavement by a man bent on her ruin. The sweet privilege of fatherhood is portrayed as worthless as an old rag that can be cast off at will.

This absolute vacuum of nobility, of feelings and principles no higher than animals, is fed to our children daily. There is no break.

It was not noble thought that changed the term housewife to domestic engineer. It was not noble thought that changed chairman or chairwoman to chairperson. It is not noble debate that forbids our congressmen to turn in a timely annual budget or that prevents the payment of our nation's just debts before they become our grandchildren's burden. Noble thought did not create our penal system.

Noble thought is what moms do when they sit down with a child to do homework. It is what Boy Scout leaders do when they try one more time to make an Eagle out of a boy. It is what Girl Scout leaders do when they tell a haggard mom, "We'll pick her up and get her home tonight."

NOBLE THOUGHTS

It is what a dad does when he shows a kid how to worm the hook. It is what a tired father does to see that junior gets to go to college. It is what Army wives do when someone else's husband doesn't make it home from a mission.

It is the sacrifice a community makes to help one of their own who has fallen on hard times.

Noble thought is absent of selfishness, greed or ulterior motive. Noble thought is love without condition; it is patience without reason. It has in its core a long-term purpose, one which usually outlives the thinker.

Noble families are the primary source of such inspiration.

Mom and Dad, teach your children noble thoughts and principles. Live nobly. They will love you forever. Your children and grandchildren shall be the salt of the earth and perhaps lead this world from some of its darkness.

Your young men shall be brave and faithful because of you. Your young women shall be the sacred watchmen of the principles you teach. They shall teach those principles to their own children. They shall know who they are. They shall know real happiness and the price required to obtain it. They shall rise up and call you great.

I believe angels take note and God is pleased by such families. I believe God is always on the side of nobility.

THE END

1969 12 06 Grandma Hazel Marsh & L/CPL Dan Kingsley

NOBLE THOUGHTS

About the Author

Dan Kingsley is a free-lance writer and columnist. Throughout his military careers—six years in the U.S. Marine Corps and 17 years as a U.S. Army Aviation Warrant Officer (Cobra & OH-58 A/C), he has never stopped writing. As jobs and careers changed, he poured into his writing all he learned in business and family life, which really did include six children, a three-legged dog, and the enterprise of raising pigs as a hobby.

He considers himself the World's Leading Authority on "how to raise six kids without a single murder." After nearly three decades of writing his thoughts in various publications, he is finally sharing his wisdom and wise cracks with the public in this book; others to follow.

Kingsley now makes his home in Buffalo, New York, where the Beef on Weck is King and the Chicken Wings are the best in the world.

He welcomes your remarks or questions via e-mail: scoutdriver74@gmail.com

.

Printed in the USA
CPSIA information can be obtained
at www.ICGtesting.com
BVHW050208160823
668592BV00004B/21